Now, What Do You Believe?

Now, What Do You Believe?

Gregory R. Wille

Horizon Publishers
Springville, Utah

ISBN 13: 978-0-88290-840-3

Published by Horizon Publishers, an imprint of Cedar Fort, Inc., 2373 W. 700 S., Springville, UT, 84663
Distributed by Cedar Fort, Inc. www.cedarfort.com

LIBRARY OF CONGRESS CATALOGING-IN-PUBLICATION DATA

Wille, Gregory R., 1947–
  Now, what do you believe? / Gregory R. Wille.
    p. cm.
  ISBN 978-0-88290-840-3
  1. Church of Jesus Christ of Latter-day Saints—Doctrines. I. Title.
  BX8635.3.W545 2007
  230'.9332—dc22
                              2007052254

Cover design by Nicole Williams
Cover design © 2008 by Lyle Mortimer

Printed in the United States of America

10 9 8 7 6 5 4 3 2 1

Printed on acid-free paper

Contents

Acknowledgments

Many of the quotations from early Christian writers and other historical notations cited in this book have been borrowed from the original research and writings of the late Dr. James L. Barker as found in his scholarly work *Apostasy from the Divine Church*. Without his extraordinary research efforts and gospel insights, this book would not be what it is. I extend a special word of thanks to this great man.

Thanks must also be extended to great Church leaders and authors such as Elders Bruce R. McConkie, Joseph F. McConkie, LeGrand Richards, and a host of others. I have borrowed liberally from their writings and wisdom, without which this book would be greatly lacking.

Finally, a special thanks must go to my wife, Shelley; my sister Patty; and my friend Noma. Their suggestions for improving this book have been extremely helpful and greatly appreciated.

Preface

This book is not an authorized or official publication of The Church of Jesus Christ of Latter-day Saints. It is simply one man's attempt to explain a few of his LDS beliefs and to share his personal testimony with family members, friends, and neighbors.

In general terms, the book has been written with the intent, and hope, of bringing souls to Christ; for it is He, our Lord and Savior, who brings souls to God.

In more specific terms, my purpose in writing this book has been to strengthen the testimonies of the individual members of the Church who read it.

Perhaps there will be some not of our faith who are curious about LDS teachings and might choose to read this book. If so, what you read here will introduce you to a few of our basic beliefs, and will help you understand where true joy, happiness, and all of the magnificent blessings that God has prepared for you might be found.

The Great Apostasy

As young LDS missionaries go out into the world to present the restored gospel message to those of other faiths, and sometimes to those of no faith at all, they speak only briefly and in passing of the Great Apostasy or falling away from Christian truths that took place during the Middle and Dark Ages of history. They realize that, without question, the least effective method for teaching the truths of the restored gospel is to argue or "Bible-bash" over beliefs and doctrines held by others, or to otherwise create a spirit of contention during a religious discussion. So, obviously the missionaries take a very positive approach instead, generally neither bringing up nor criticizing the beliefs of other churches or philosophies, but rather testifying and teaching their own simple message in hopes that the Spirit will touch the hearts of those willing to listen. This is the most effective and truly inspired approach to take for those who are open-minded and spiritually prepared to receive this divine message.

There are many people, however, who have soft hearts but closed minds. Although they are living very good lives and are thus spiritually prepared to receive the truth, they are not socially, or perhaps not mentally prepared to receive it. This, unfortunately, constitutes the vast majority of investigators. Such individuals seldom make it past the first missionary discussion. Why not? Either for fear of breaking family religious traditions and thus offending or disappointing parents or friends, or because they are intellectually unable to see the need for a divine restoration to earth of original Christian truths. Knowing relatively little about ancient Christian church history, or original Christian teachings, they can see nothing wrong with their own church—in fact, their church seems just fine. What need is there for such things as modern-day living prophets, apostles, divine revelation, and a "restoration" of original gospel truths anyway? Doesn't their own church already possess the truth? Why should they do something so drastic as to join a different church?

Now, as a person reads through this book, I believe they will come to recognize such a need—the need for a restoration of Christ's original Church and gospel to the earth. This will become clear to them as they learn of the Great Apostasy that did indeed take place during medieval times and continues to occur in our own modern time. In this book we will take a look at some of the ancient, original, and now restored teachings of Christ as found within The Church of Jesus Christ of Latter-day Saints. We will compare these teachings of divine origin with those very confusing man-made teachings commonly being taught in the world today.

A CANDLE IN THE NIGHT

If you were to light a candle and place it on the front porch of your home at noonday, how many passersby would even notice it? Probably very few. If, however, you were to light that same candle and place it on your front porch on a very dark, moonless night, how many would notice it? Certainly everyone who walked by. During daylight hours, the light generated from the candle is scarcely noticeable or needed—but at night the usefulness of the light it generates, illuminating the porch and a portion of the front yard, is obvious to all.

In a similar manner, when the light radiating from the pure gospel of Christ is held up in, and compared to, the dark, false, illogical philosophies and counterfeit doctrines of men, the truth is much easier to discern and its benefits so obvious to all.

When our Heavenly Father and His Beloved Son restored to earth the truths of the pure gospel of Christ, in a sense they lit a candle in the night. No, it was not a huge bonfire that would immediately draw billions of people to it. Rather, it was just a little candle that we are told would draw a relatively few truth-seeking, discerning, wise souls to it (see Matthew 7:13–14). In this book I will be holding up that little candle and comparing the light flowing from it to the mists of doctrinal darkness that surround it on every side.

My prayer is that each of us will recognize, embrace, and eternally benefit from those divine rays of light streaming from it. Then, in turn, we can become beacons of light unto the world, helping all other sincere seekers in their quest for pure and undefiled truth.

GRANDPA'S FAITH

I grew up in the western suburbs of Chicago, living a somewhat simple, unremarkable life, although blessed with quite an unusual, wonderful family. At the age of fifteen, I had several significant spiritual experiences that greatly increased my faith in God, in the Savior, and in the truth of the teachings of the LDS Church. Following my freshman year of college, at the age of nineteen, I sought and received a mission call from the leaders of the Church. I was assigned to serve for two years in the magnificent land of Australia.

Saying good-bye to family and friends, I flew from Chicago to Salt Lake City for missionary training. While most ministers of religion in modern Christian churches today study theology for at least four years, receiving a college degree in it, my formal training lasted only one week. My training was simple, but it was sufficient, for I had been blessed throughout my young life with a strong religious foundation—the wonderful examples and teachings of kind and loving righteous parents, Sunday School teachers, and other dedicated Church leaders and teachers. Nevertheless, being so young and inexperienced in the ways of the world made me think of the apostle Paul's statement: "For ye see your calling, brethren, how that not many wise men after the flesh, not many mighty, not many noble, are called: But God hath chosen the foolish things of the world to confound the wise; and God hath chosen the weak things of the world to confound the things which are mighty" (1 Corinthians 1:26–27).

Certainly the lowly fisherman Peter and the tentmaker Paul were considered fools by the religious leaders of their day. But God could make weak things strong, and if He could do it with them, then He could do it with me—I considered myself the weakest and the most foolish of all His servants.

After completing my week of study and training, I was permitted to leave the Mission Home late Sunday afternoon and spend my final evening, before leaving the United States, with my grandpa. Upon retirement, my grandpa had moved from Chicago to Salt Lake City. He was a widower living alone, my grandmother having passed on some eight years earlier. This visit would prove to be a truly wonderful experience for me, for during my entire life I had never had a single moment alone with my grandpa. It seems that it had always been at family gatherings that I would see him. This evening his attention would be focused on only me.

Following dinner, we retired to the living room and began to talk. As I was a young man preparing to leave for the mission field, as might be expected, our conversation turned to religion.

I asked Grandpa about his younger years and how he had come to join the Church, for I knew from my parents that he was a convert to the LDS faith. He told me that when he was a young man, close to my own age, he was attending theological school and studying to become an ordained minister in a large and popular Protestant sect. One evening he found himself standing outside the entrance of a large tent, looking in at a religious revival being held by another Protestant faith. Soon he noticed a man standing beside him who was also peering through the doorway, observing the proceedings taking place inside.

My grandpa and this stranger began talking, commenting back and forth about the proceedings they were watching. Grandpa admired the enthusiasm of the members of this sect he was observing, but he felt that his own church possessed the truth while the teachings of this other sect were quite off base on several points of doctrine. As they conversed, Grandpa soon learned that this man to whom he was talking was a local leader of the Mormon Church in the city. Just before departing, this stranger invited Grandpa to attend church services the next Sunday, and out of sheer curiosity Grandpa accepted his offer.

Grandpa said that during his youth he had not heard too much about the LDS faith, but what little he had heard was all negative. Family and friends referred to members of this church as the despised Mormons. The few pamphlets he had read about Mormonism made this Church seem truly bizarre. He wondered what sort of people could possibly believe such strange things. He was curious to find out. Perhaps he could help some of these poor deluded people see the error of their ways and straighten them out.

The next Sunday at church services, Grandpa was quite surprised to discover that these Mormons did not seem strange at all. They were very pleasant and did not appear to be fanatical, delusional, or stupid. In fact, they all seemed quite normal and intelligent. After the meeting, he was introduced to some missionaries and agreed to attend some discussions where he would learn more about the Church. At this point he still very much believed that his own church contained the truth and that LDS teachings were far out in left field somewhere. Being quite the Bible scholar, he was still planning on straightening out these naive, foolish missionaries. Little did he know at that time that it would be him, not them, who would end up being straightened out.

THE LOVING NATURE OF GOD

The leaders of Grandpa's former church taught that God is an extremely loving and kind divine being. However, in the next breath these ministers and professors of religion would then teach doctrines that made God appear to be just the opposite—extremely cruel, merciless, and even quite barbaric in nature.

Although my grandpa felt that his church contained so much that was true, he wondered about the doctrines of original sin and infant baptism. He knew that as an ordained minister in his church, he would be required to baptize little babies—something he felt a little uncomfortable about doing. According to the teachings of his former church, every person is born into this life stained by the so-called original sin of Adam. The only way this sin can be removed from a person is by baptism. If a tiny infant died before being baptized, and thus had not had this sin removed, it was unworthy to enter heaven and was damned by God to suffer an eternity in hell. Grandpa had always wondered, is this a just and loving God? A divine being who condemns and eternally punishes helpless little babies for a sin committed by someone else?

From his discussions with the missionaries, Grandpa learned the truth—that just the opposite is true. God loves little children. He does not punish them. As the Savior made clear, unless we ourselves become pure like a little child, we will not enter the kingdom of God.

And what about hell itself? According to the teachings of his church, hell was a place where the wicked go at the time of death. It consisted of "fire and brimstone," where unrepentant sinners had their flesh continually burned by fire but were never totally consumed. Is this a just and loving God? A being who delights in physically torturing unbaptized babies and other men, women, and children, burning their flesh with fire forever and ever and ever with no end? To Grandpa, such a being sounded far more cruel than the most evil of mortal villains in our world. Such a doctrine seemed so totally inconsistent with the concept of the just, loving, and merciful God that he believed in.

Imagine how you would feel if rumors were going around your community that defamed your character, being spread by those who professed to be your friends. They were telling others that you were sending servants down to the basement of your home, there to torture your beloved child. In truth, just the opposite was true—you loved your child with all of your heart and spent much of your day holding her close and pampering her. Imagine the hurt and then the great anger you would feel toward those so-called friends who were spreading these terrible lies. Imagine the disgust you would feel for those who actually believed these lies and repeated these falsehoods to still others. Now imagine what our Heavenly Father must feel at His perfectly loving nature being slandered in just such a manner.

GRACE ALONE

As still another example of a modern doctrine or creed that tends to vilify God, consider the doctrine of being saved by grace alone, a doctrine that is popular in so many Christian sects of our day. This doctrine was central to the beliefs of Grandpa's particular church. According to this doctrine, grace does not represent those many gifts that Christ freely offers to *all* of God's children, such as His Atonement for sin. Grandpa was taught that grace is something that God quite randomly bestows upon only a few of His children while purposely withholding it from the vast majority of mankind. His selection of a few individuals to receive His grace is apparently based upon nothing more than some divine whim. In other words, nothing that you or I personally can do, either for good or for evil, has anything to do with His choice of whom He selects to save or damn.

According to this doctrine, grace represents some kind of irresistible force through which God draws a few individuals to Him. These particularly lucky individuals that He has selected for salvation He forces to believe in Jesus Christ, thus making them worthy of salvation. No individual freedom of choice is allowed.[1]

In practice, according to this doctrine, if a man comes to believe that Jesus is his Savior, and publicly confesses this belief, he obviously has come under the saving power of God's grace, and his salvation is thus assured, nothing else being required of him.

One of the many questions this doctrine begs to be answered, however, is, if God can bestow grace upon whomsoever He desires, why doesn't He just give His grace to everyone, force all to believe in Christ, and thus save all of mankind? If he purposely withholds His grace from most of mankind, obviously He must not really care about the welfare of the great majority of His children, completely forsaking them to suffer the pains and torments of an endless hell. Did God really create the vast majority of mankind with no other thought in mind than to temporarily place them upon the earth for a few minutes, months, or years and then ship them off to endless, physical torture in hellfire, with no freedom of choice on their part to influence their own destiny? Is this a just and loving God?

TEN MEN STUCK IN QUICKSAND

To illustrate this point more clearly, imagine you are taking a walk in the woods and come upon a group of ten men who had been hiking together and have accidentally fallen into quicksand. You can see that each one is slowly sinking and is just a few minutes away from death. You observe a tree branch lying on the ground nearby, which you could easily hold out to each man and pull him free. You have the means and ability to save these men's lives. Would you do it? Of course you would.

Now, if Christ had come upon these same ten men struggling in the quicksand, would He pull them out? Well, according to this doctrine, nine times out of ten, no, He wouldn't. It's not that He really *desires* that each of these men sink to their death. Actually, He has no feelings for them one way or the other and is simply allowing justice to take its natural course. He is the only hope these men have for rescue. He has the means and ability to save each and every one of them—but He chooses not to. No, wait, He is thinking about it. Maybe He will save one of them. Maybe not. Oh, all right, He decides to save one. Let's see, which one should He choose? Oh, it doesn't matter. He decides to pick the man with the red hair. But then again, what about the husky man with the black hair and mustache? Such a difficult choice . . . Oh well, He finally decides to rescue the man with the red hair after all. What a lucky fellow he is!

Apparently God cares but little for any of these men. He created them all as sinners, and He would just as soon watch them all suffer and die as to rescue any one of them. In order to show that there is a little bit of kindness in His heart, however, He does decide to reach out and save one of them so that this man can spend the rest of eternity singing praises to Him.

This is the God of much of modern Christendom—a God who is praised in church for His kindness and mercy in extending His tree branch to one lucky sinner, while at the same time turning His back and allowing nine others to sink to their death. One wonders just what sort of uncaring, unmerciful, sadistic being this God really is. We are fortunate indeed that such a God does not really exist!

From his studies of LDS teachings, Grandpa learned that the true God of heaven, the God that really does exist, holds out His branch, or grace, to everyone—*all* will receive a chance to hear His pure, saving gospel message at some point in time. He loves and cares immensely for each and every one of us. He knows us individually and by name. His Atonement for sin is available for the benefit of every one of God's children. But because they are given the freedom of choice, many will choose to sink to their death in the quicksand of sin rather than grasp the hand that is being held out to rescue and lift them to eternal life. It is not Christ who turns His back on sinners; it is we as sinners who so often turn our face away from Him, refusing to take his hand. He weeps at the loss of any soul.

FALSE DOCTRINES AND SOCIETY

Now, of course, Grandpa knew that virtually all modern Christian churches encourage their members to live good and righteous lives and to follow the example of the Savior. Unfortunately, however, the ministers of many of these modern churches, including his own, would then tell their members that although they *should* be obedient to God's commands— that is, do good works—it really isn't necessary to do so, because good works play no part in the attainment of salvation. For a man is chosen by God and saved by grace alone. So what does this place in a person's mind? Why bother to put forth any effort to be obedient to God or to do good when such effort is of absolutely no benefit or of any consequence to me? God will not bless me for my good works, nor will He punish me for my lack of good works. So why do them? As long as I have been chosen to receive God's grace and I profess a belief in Christ, I will be saved—nothing else is required.

The population of the United States today is approximately 80 percent

Christian, and yet most observers agree that morally and spiritually the country is degenerating and rapidly spiraling downward. Some religious leaders are beginning to lay at least part of the blame for this on the popular doctrine of salvation by grace alone. One such thoughtful Protestant minister notes:

> The more I have examined Jesus' public ministry and His dealings with inquirers, the more apprehensive I have become about the methods and content of contemporary evangelism. On a disturbing number of fronts, the message being proclaimed today is not the gospel according to Jesus.
>
> The gospel in vogue today holds forth a false hope to sinners. It promises them they can have eternal life yet continue to live in rebellion against God. Indeed, it encourages people to claim Jesus as Savior yet defer until later the commitment to obey Him as Lord. It promises salvation from hell but not necessarily freedom from iniquity. It offers false security to people who revel in the sins of the flesh and spurn the way of holiness. By separating faith from faithfulness, it leaves the impression that intellectual assent is as valid as wholehearted obedience to the truth. Thus the good news of Christ has given way to the bad news of insidious easy-believism that makes no moral demands on the lives of sinners. It is not the same message Jesus proclaimed.
>
> This new gospel has spawned a generation of professing Christians whose behavior often is indistinguishable from the rebellion of the unregenerate.[2]

In other words, due to this very popular modern doctrine of salvation by grace alone, it is becoming more and more difficult to distinguish between the behavior of a modern-day Christian and that of a non-Christian or even an atheist. Of course, what else might be expected from those who have been taught all their lives that in order to reap the blessings of salvation you simply need to have faith—you don't need to be faithful?

Now, don't get me wrong. Certainly there are many wonderful people that believe this doctrine who are living very good and honorable lives. But the truth of the matter is obvious: they live good lives in spite of their belief in this doctrine, not because of it. On the other hand, many millions of people are living far less faithful lives than they otherwise might because of their belief in this popular but very false and dangerous doctrine.

In modern Christianity, we find doctrines of infant damnation, physical torture forever in hellfire, and forced salvation or damnation based upon nothing more than simply the divine whims and amazing grace of God. These were but three examples of doctrines taught in Grandpa's church that made God appear so cruel, unfair, and merciless—doctrines that Grandpa had to admit were both unreasonable and could not possibly be true. Later we will examine these and many other doctrines more closely and learn that God is not at all the merciless barbarian that these teachings would indicate. In fact, we will see that any religious doctrine that would make you question or doubt the perfectly just, loving, kind, and merciful nature of our Heavenly Father is built upon nothing but sheer misconception and error—such slanderous doctrines are simply not true.

GRANDPA'S DECISION

As Grandpa continued his studies with the missionaries and began to compare LDS teachings with those of his own faith, he was surprised to discover many other teachings and practices in his church that did not seem to make sense or were not in harmony with original Christian teachings or practices. From his studies, he could certainly see the need for a restoration of Christ's original, pure teachings to the earth—a restoration of truth that he learned from the missionaries had indeed already occurred.

Within a few short months' time, through study and much prayer, Grandpa became convinced of the truth of what the missionaries had been teaching him. He desired to be baptized into The Church of Jesus Christ of Latter-day Saints. When his father learned of this desire, he flew into a fury, threatening to disown him if he did so. Grandpa tried to explain to his father what the Church taught, but his father's mind was closed and he refused to listen. Grandpa was further told that if he joined the LDS Church, his bags would be packed and he could pick up all of his personal belongings and leave the house the next time he ventured home.

At the college where he was studying, when the teachers and administrators got wind of his plans, they called him into a special meeting. They pulled out several anti-Mormon pamphlets and started reading to Grandpa. Among other things, they read a story about how Joseph Smith, the founder of the LDS faith, had attempted to deceive the people of his day. They claimed that on one occasion, he had pretended to walk on water while actually walking on planks of wood that had been hidden just under the water's surface.

When Grandpa told me that story, I simply burst out laughing. I had heard many bizarre, false stories made up about the Prophet Joseph Smith and about LDS teachings, but that one took the cake. Joseph Smith pretending to walk on water! It was utterly amazing to me to what lengths people would go in distorting the truth and even making up outright lies to discourage people from finding out the true teachings of the LDS Church.

Well, try as they might, the professors and administrators could not sway Grandpa in his decision. It was too late—he already knew the truth, and he knew that what they were telling him was not true.

When Grandpa joined The Church of Jesus Christ of Latter-day Saints, he sacrificed his good standing in his family, lost many of his friends, and in essence threw away an advanced education along with the means to obtain a comfortable livelihood for himself and his family. He lived through the Great Depression of the 1930s without the benefit of an advanced education to help support his family, suffering much as a result. Perhaps the most difficult thing for him to endure, however, was that his father never forgave him for his decision. As sad and as difficult as that was to bear, Grandpa's first and foremost allegiance was still to God. Although he greatly loved his father, he loved God more, for he knew, as the Savior Himself taught, "He that loveth father or mother more than me is not worthy of me" (Matthew 10:37). His greatest desire was to be worthy of the Savior's love.

Easing the pain somewhat was the fact that he never lost the love of his dear, sweet mother. Some months after his baptism into the Church, she related to him that she had had a very vivid and remarkable dream in which she saw her husband and their minister standing covered in a dark cloud, while my grandpa was standing in the light. Although her husband would not allow her to learn about the Church, somehow she felt confident God was pleased with her son's decision. Years later, as he told me of his conversion, Grandpa felt certain his mother, having long ago passed from this life, had accepted the restored gospel in the spirit world.

That would be the last time I ever saw my grandpa, for he would pass away a year later, while I was serving on my mission in Australia. I will never forget that evening spent with him and will forever be grateful for the sacrifices he made in his life, from which I personally have so greatly benefited.

NOTES

1. Although many Protestant sects today believe in the "irresistible" nature of grace, many others do not. Nearly all modern Christian sects, however, share in a general confusion over the doctrine of God's grace. We will discuss this principle of grace in more depth in a later chapter of this book.

2. John F. MacArthur Jr., *The Gospel According to Jesus* (Grand Rapids: Zondervan Publishing, 1988), 15–16, 85. Used by permission.

Introduction

As Latter-day Saints, we are all familiar with Joseph Smith's First Vision, wherein this young fourteen-year-old farm boy sought guidance from his Heavenly Father in humble prayer, seeking to know which church was right—that is, of all the many contending Christian sects that existed in his day, which one was God's *true* church? Which church should he join? In answer to his humble prayer, Joseph received a glorious vision in which he was visited by two heavenly beings—God the Father and His beloved Son, Jesus Christ—appearing together before him, side by side.

At this time, in answer to his question, the Savior informed Joseph that he must not join any of these churches, for none of them was His—indeed, they were all wrong in so many of their beliefs and teachings. He was informed that a great apostasy or "falling away" from the Savior's divine church and gospel had taken place during the Middle and Dark Ages. Although His true church and pure gospel had been lost for many centuries, both were soon to be restored to earth.

As Joseph later went forth proclaiming those doctrines that he had received directly from the Savior and from heavenly messengers later sent to him by the Savior, those listening to him found answers to their questions unlike anything they had ever heard before.

In the following pages are presented several such questions. We will answer these questions from the original teachings of Christ as restored to earth through the Prophet Joseph Smith. To show just how unique and truly enlightening were the doctrines that Joseph received directly from the Savior and from His divinely appointed messengers, we will compare these LDS beliefs with doctrines commonly taught in modern Christian faiths. By doing so, just as my grandfather came to realize, we too will learn how clear one's views suddenly appear when a light is held up to darkness!

Let's begin our discussion by posing a question that had concerned and bothered my grandfather for years—a question that he finally found a reasonable answer to as he studied the teachings of the restored gospel of Jesus Christ.

Section I
Life After Death

QUESTION #1

As a practicing Christian, I have been taught that only those who believe in Christ and accept His gospel can be "saved" in heaven. If this is true, then what is the fate of the literally billions of people who, over the course of this earth's history, have lived and died never having even heard the name of Christ, let alone having been taught His gospel? Have they no chance of ever returning to God's presence? Are they forever doomed?

ORIGINAL CHRISTIAN TEACHINGS

Christ taught, "I am the way, the truth, and the life: no man cometh unto the Father, but by me" (John 14:6). He is the Savior of the entire world, and only by accepting and living His gospel can anyone ever hope to enter the presence of the Father.

So, how are people to learn of the Savior and His pure gospel? How can they obtain this gospel and thus come to know what they must do to return to the Father? The Savior Himself, after His resurrection, just before His formal ascension into heaven, gave these instructions to His disciples: "And he said unto them, Go ye into all the world, and *preach the gospel to every creature*. He that believeth and is baptized will be saved; but he that believeth not will be damned" (Mark 16:15–16; italics added).

The gospel of Jesus Christ must be preached to every creature! Of course, even as Jesus was uttering these words, there were people in various parts of the earth who were dying—people passing into the next life who had never heard of Christ or His gospel. How could Jesus' command be fulfilled? How could *every* human being be given the opportunity to hear His gospel preached?

In the early Christian church, it was taught that upon death, the immortal spirits of all men and women leave their physical bodies and journey to a place known as the spirit world, there to await the resurrection and their final judgment. As individuals enter this world of spirits, a preliminary or partial judgment occurs—the "sheep" are separated from the "goats." That is, those who have accepted and faithfully lived Christ's pure gospel (the sheep) are gathered together and dwell in a state of great happiness. All others (the goats) go to a much different place that is figuratively described in the scriptures as the spirit prison. No, these individuals do not dwell behind steel bars. Rather, they are prisoners who are bound and held back from progressing further by either their own ignorance, sins, false beliefs, or disbelief. As the Savior Himself indicated, only a humble acceptance of truth can set a man free from this spiritual bondage. (See John 8:32.)

During the early years of Christianity, it was taught that in the justice and fairness of God, those who do not have the opportunity to hear Christ's pure gospel message while living upon the earth will receive the opportunity in the next life, during their stay in the spirit world. This will take place prior to their resurrection and final judgment. All of God's children are to be treated fairly; all will have the chance to either accept or reject the pure, uncorrupted gospel of Christ.

It was Jesus Christ, of course, who began this work of salvation among the dead. The apostle Peter taught that following Christ's death on the cross, during the three days that His physical body lay in the tomb, the Lord's spirit journeyed into the spirit world. While there, the Savior preached the gospel to a group of individuals who had never heard this message of salvation while living upon the earth.

> For Christ also hath once suffered for sins, the just for the unjust, that he might bring us to God, being put to death in the flesh, but quickened by the Spirit: By which also *he went and preached unto the spirits in prison;* Which sometime were disobedient, when once the longsuffering of God waited in the days of Noah. (1 Peter 3:18–20; italics added)

> For for this cause was *the gospel preached also to them that are dead*, that they might be judged according to men in the flesh, but live according to God in the spirit. (1 Peter 4:6; italics added)

Christian leaders of the first two centuries AD confirmed these truths in their writings, declaring that not only Christ, but other priesthood holders also, continued preaching after death, ministering to the souls of men and women while dwelling in the spirit world.

> It was for this reason, too, that the Lord descended into the regions beneath the earth, preaching his advent there also, and (declaring) the remission of sins received by those who believe in him. (Saint Irenaeus, AD 123–203)[1]

> Again, from the words of Jeremiah, they have also cut this: "The Lord God, the Holy One of Israel, remembered his dead who were sleeping in the tomb of the earth, and he descended unto them to announce the good news (gospel) of their salvation. (Justin Martyr, AD 100–166)[2]

> These apostles and teachers, who preached the name of the Son of God having fallen asleep in the power and faith of the Son of God, preached also to those who had fallen asleep before them, and themselves gave to them the seal of preaching. (Shepherd of Hermas)[3]

> The idea that hearing the gospel and baptism is necessary for the salvation of the righteous dead of pre-Christian times is common.[4]

MEDIEVAL AND MODERN CHRISTIAN TEACHINGS

As centuries passed, a clear understanding of that intermediary state of existence between death and the resurrection, known as the spirit world, became lost or rejected. As a result, it began to be taught by medieval Christian leaders that God would mercilessly condemn and punish many millions and even billions of His children for not accepting and living His gospel, while providing absolutely no opportunity for them to even hear it preached! This teaching led to the conclusion that God had created the vast majority of mankind with no other intention than to temporarily place them upon the earth for a relatively few years and then send them off to an endless hell.

This doctrine has come to be called exclusivism—a belief that those who do not accept Christ while living upon the earth are forever excluded from God's presence in heaven.

Today, very conservative evangelical Christian churches teach, and correctly so, that a person can only return to the Father's presence through

Christ. Christ Himself, of course, very clearly taught this truth. Sadly, however, members of these churches have no knowledge of the intermediary life each of us will temporarily experience in the spirit world and of the great missionary work that is taking place there. During a lunch hour, I once asked a coworker of mine, a member of one of these churches, "What is the eternal fate of those who die without any knowledge of Christ while living on the earth?" As I recall, his answer was quite short and directly to the point: "They reside forever in hell." When I questioned him further about the unfairness and cruelty of such a fate, he replied, "Well, God is God. He chooses whoever He wants to live with Him in heaven and all the rest are consigned to hell. We are in no position to question or judge His justice."

Well, like it or not, I guess I can judge well enough. For if this commonly held belief of large portions of modern Christendom was actually true, how terribly cruel, merciless, and unfair our Heavenly Father would be. Just imagine, God forever punishing a man for not accepting a gospel that he did not even know existed.

Earlier in this book, we briefly discussed several doctrines taught in my grandpa's former church that he recognized could not possibly be true. These were doctrines that portrayed God as an unfair and cruel being: the doctrines of infant damnation; the eternal physical torture of men, women, and children in hellfire; and God's arbitrary and random bestowal of "amazing grace" upon a lucky few while at the same time purposely withholding His love and grace from the vast majority of His children. Exclusivism, as described above, is just one more example of a doctrine taught in many modern Christian churches today that can be added to this list. It is just one more modern, man-made doctrine that, quite frankly, portrays God as an uncaring, merciless, tyrannical beast.

A second, more mainstream or moderate division of modern Christendom holds a much different belief on this matter. These churches, such as the Roman Catholic[5] and Orthodox faiths, teach that a belief in Jesus Christ is not actually necessary in order to enter God's presence (this they believe in spite of Christ's teachings to the contrary). They teach that through the grace of Christ, not only does He save good Christians, but He also chooses some non-Christians to save as well. Simply because of Christ's loving nature, He is willing to save a few who have never accepted Him as their Savior nor the truths of His divine gospel. This doctrine is called inclusivism. Other non-evangelical or more mainstream Protestant sects are uncertain and vary widely in their beliefs on this matter—some including and some excluding non-Christians from heaven.

Very liberal modern Christian sects open the gates to heaven even wider than do those preaching inclusivism. They teach what is known as pluralism or universalism. Contrary to Christ's teachings, they say that there is not simply *one* "strait and narrow path" leading to heaven. Putting aside what the Bible teaches, they say that there are many different paths back to the Father's presence. Good people of all religious persuasions—Christian, Jewish, Muslim, Hindu, Shinto, Buddhist, and so on—*all* are permitted to enter back into the Father's presence whether they believe the truth or not. Apparently Christ is the Savior for Christians, but not the Savior of the world.

These three viewpoints put forth by various modern Christian churches—exclusivism, inclusivism, and pluralism—are doctrines that are actually quite unique and different from one another. There is one shared characteristic or thread running through them, however, namely: all three are false, man-made theories. They simply are not true. Such doctrines were never taught by Christ, by His apostles, or by any other Church leaders during the early centuries of the Christian era. All three errors are a result of a loss of knowledge concerning the spirit world and of God's both perfectly just and perfectly loving nature.

CHRIST'S ORIGINAL TEACHINGS RESTORED TO JOSEPH SMITH

Through the Prophet Joseph Smith, God once again revealed the truth that He is "no respecter of persons" (Acts 10:34). In other words, He is perfectly just and fair, interacting with all of His children on equal terms. He loves every one of His children and has provided in His plan of salvation a way that all will eventually be given the opportunity to hear—and to accept or to reject—the pure and uncorrupted gospel of Jesus Christ and those blessings of salvation that only the Savior offers. God could never be so cruel or merciless as to condemn or punish any one of His children for not accepting or living a gospel that they never even knew existed! Those who do not have the opportunity to receive the pure and uncorrupted gospel in this life will have the opportunity in the next life.

When men and women eventually stand before the final judgment bar of God, none will be able to claim that they have been treated unfairly. Each will recognize and admit that they were given the opportunity to receive the Savior's pure gospel and will vividly recall their own acceptance or rejection of these blessings.

I testify to you, dear reader, that these basic Christian teachings, lost from mankind's understanding for so many centuries, have been revealed anew by the Lord through a latter-day prophet of God. God really is perfectly fair and merciful in His judgments—all are given the chance to receive His pure and undefiled gospel. So also, however, is God perfectly just—only those who qualify by accepting the Savior and by living His pure gospel are permitted to enter the Father's presence—there are no free passes into the highest of heavens for some randomly picked, unbelieving, lucky few.

The principles of the pure and uncorrupted gospel of Jesus Christ, when properly understood, make perfect sense. God really *does* love all of His children. He really *is* just and fair. Every one of His children *will* receive an opportunity to hear and accept His pure gospel. I know these things to be true.

Now, What Do You Believe?

If you were asked, how would you answer this question: What is the eternal fate of those men and women who live and die without ever having even heard the name of Christ while living upon the earth? (Mentally, check one of these three answers.)

Modern: I agree with the teachings of many modern Christian churches that teach that such individuals are automatically consigned to eternal suffering in hell. Christ taught that no one can enter God's presence without believing on Him. To us it may sound unfair that billions of people are never given a chance to learn about Christ or His gospel, but God is God and He can do whatever He wants with His creations. We cannot fully understand all of His mysterious ways.

Modern: I agree with those many other modern Christian churches that teach that such individuals, if they have lived basically good lives, can still go to heaven to live with God. A belief in Jesus Christ is not actually necessary for a man or woman to enter His presence. There are many pathways into heaven.

Ancient and Restored: I agree with the teachings of *original* Christianity that no man or woman can enter back into the Father's presence except through Christ. He is the Son of God and Savior of the world. Because of God's perfectly just and merciful nature, He has made certain that each of His children will receive the opportunity to learn of Christ and to receive His pure, uncorrupted gospel. Those who do not receive that opportunity during their life on earth will receive that chance while living in the spirit world, prior to their resurrection and final judgment.

QUESTION #2

I consider myself a basically good person, although not overly religious. I was baptized as an infant, but now as an adult I seldom pray, read from the scriptures, or seek forgiveness from God for my mistakes. To please my wife, I occasionally attend church services on Sunday, but I rarely think about religion during the rest of the week. While I do believe in Jesus Christ, I guess some might call me lukewarm in my devotion to Him. I sometimes take the Lord's name in vain when I'm angry. But on the positive side, I am a very honest person, a good provider for my family, and a kind and loving father to my children. In the next life, will someone like me go to heaven or to hell?

ORIGINAL CHRISTIAN TEACHINGS

During the early years of Christianity, it was taught that following their temporary stay in the spirit world, *all* men and women will be resurrected with a perfect, immortal physical body and then brought to stand before the bar of God to be judged. The rewards and punishments men and women inherit at this time will greatly vary, based upon their faith in Christ and their obedience, or lack of obedience, to God's commandments. Those who have qualified for salvation will inherit one of three very different heavens or rewards, based upon their worthiness.

The Savior taught, "In my Father's house are many mansions" (John 14:2). That is to say, while many may enter Heavenly Father's house, or heaven, not everyone will receive the same mansion or reward. Along these same lines, the apostle Paul spoke of not one, but of *three* very different types of resurrected bodies with which men and women would be raised in the next life, comparing these different glorious bodies to the glory of the stars, the moon, and the sun. And even among these he noted that "one star differeth from another star in glory," indicating that a reward or punishment would be tailor-made for each individual. (See 1 Corinthians 15:40–42.) In our courts on earth, a man who is guilty of a traffic violation receives a much different punishment than a man guilty of murder. Is God, a perfect and all-knowing Being, any less capable of meting out justice with perfect fairness than are mortal men who are in charge of earthly tribunals?

The apostle Paul also spoke of a man who had once been lifted up and allowed to see the third or highest of heavens: "I knew a man in Christ above fourteen years ago, (whether in the body, I cannot tell; or whether out of the body, I cannot tell: God knoweth;) such an one caught up to the *third heaven*. And I knew such a man, (whether in the body, or out of the body, I cannot tell: God knoweth;) How that he was caught up into *paradise*, and heard unspeakable words, which it is not lawful for man to utter" (2 Corinthians 12:2–4; italics added).

Obviously, since there is a third heaven of which Paul speaks, there must also be a first and a second heaven or degree of reward. In their writings, other early Christian leaders also spoke of three very different heavens or degrees of reward that men and women would inherit in the life to come, based upon their worthiness.

> (They say, moreover), that there is this distinction between the habitation of those who produce an hundred-fold, and that of those who produce thirty-fold; for the *first* will be taken up into the *heavens*, the *second* will dwell in *paradise*, the *last [third]* will inhabit the *city*; and it was on this account the Lord declared, "In my Father's house are many mansions." For all things belong to God, who supplies all with a suitable dwelling-place; even as his Word says, that a share is allotted to all by the Father, according as each person is or will be worthy. (Saint Irenaeus)[6]

> The elect will be received into one of the *three* dwelling places signified by the figures thirty, sixty, and a hundred in the parable of the sower. (Clement of Alexandria, AD 150–211)[7]

Thus, as understood and taught by early Christian leaders, those far-less-than-valiant souls who had brought forth only "thirty-fold" would be caught up to the first heaven; those basically good men and women who had brought forth "sixty-fold" would inherit a second heaven, which Irenaeus refers to as a paradise; and those truly valiant sons and daughters of God who had accepted Christ and His pure gospel and had brought forth "an hundred-fold" would inherit the third heaven or "heavenly city," wherein God dwells, as seen and described by the apostle John. (See Revelation 21.)

The goal of every early Christian was to live worthy of an eternal inheritance in the third and highest heaven, just as it is the goal of every true and faithful Christian living upon the earth today.

MEDIEVAL AND MODERN CHRISTIAN TEACHINGS

As the Church moved into the Middle and Dark Ages, these once clearly understood teachings of the scriptures and early Church leaders would be greatly modified and changed as Christian standards of conduct were continually lowered to levels more readily acceptable to the Church's pagan converts. As a result, medieval Christian teachings eventually degenerated down to a belief in but one heaven and one hell, all "wicked" people being equally punished and all "good" people being equally rewarded, regardless of differences in individual worthiness. Figuratively speaking, someone guilty and unrepentant of a traffic ticket would be punished exactly the same as a mass murderer. And in a similar manner, those saints who had totally devoted their lives to God and to righteousness would receive no more blessings or reward in the hereafter than would those lukewarm individuals who were very casual in their devotion to God, only half-committed to righteous living.

In many ways, the acceptance of this greatly altered doctrine of one heaven and one hell, as taught even today within modern Christendom, has had a terribly negative effect upon the lives of a great many people.

> This thought has led many to feel that while their lives may not be all they should be, they are as good as, or better than, the average. Thus they feel that all will be well with them. If this doctrine be true, it is obvious that a line would have to be drawn somewhere, and the closer one came to the line the less would be the difference or distinction between those who would cross the line and enter heaven and those who would not quite qualify, and therefore would be sent to hell. [Those living lives worthy of heaven and those living lives worthy of hell might be almost identical!] Such a doctrine does not have the motivating and stimulating power to impel or encourage men to do the best they can, but rather to satisfy themselves by doing as well as the average man. Such a doctrine places no value on anything more than average devotion and obedience to the commandments of the Lord, or the development of one's talents and their useful devotion to his service.[8]

If there is only one heaven, in which God rewards the lukewarm and the truly faithful exactly the same, then why would anyone bother to put forth the effort to be fully faithful and obedient to God's commands, when absolutely nothing is to be gained by doing so?

Unfortunately, many people living today believe that a half-hearted attempt at living God's commandments is all that is required or expected of them. They unwisely believe that they will inherit all of the same blessings in eternity as those who have whole-heartedly sought after, accepted, and faithfully lived the pure gospel of Christ. According to the teachings of early Christian leaders, nothing could be further from the truth.

CHRIST'S ORIGINAL TEACHINGS RESTORED TO JOSEPH SMITH

Through the Prophet Joseph Smith the Savior revealed anew the fact that a man will eventually reap as he has sown, inheriting an eternal reward or punishment in proportion to his faith in Christ and his obedience or lack of obedience to God's laws.

A "good" person who is lukewarm in his devotion to God will certainly not be punished for sins he did not commit—but neither will he be rewarded with blessings he never actively sought nor qualified himself to receive. God has prepared a place for those who are basically good. It is not with the very wicked—but neither is it with those very righteous souls who accepted Christ's true gospel and then, aided by God's grace, tried their very best to gradually perfect their characters, to keep God's commandments, and to actively incorporate the Savior's teachings into their lives.

As part of the restoration of the pure gospel of Christ back to the earth, the Prophet Joseph Smith was permitted to see in vision the three different heavens or degrees of glory that men and women will eternally inherit in the life to come. He discovered that these three heavens vastly differ from one another in glory and in the joy and happiness experienced by those who dwell in each. Joseph also learned what the characteristics are of those individuals who dwell in each of these kingdoms—what they have done, or what they have not done, in order to obtain the reward or punishment they have received. He recorded what he learned in section 76 of the Doctrine and Covenants.

To Joseph the Lord revealed the fact that within the third and highest of these heavens, the celestial kingdom, there are several divisions or degrees of glory and reward. In order to obtain the highest of these degrees of glory (and also the highest degree of happiness and joy), a man and woman must have entered into "the new and everlasting covenant of marriage" (D&C 131:2). This ordinance of eternal marriage is performed in the holy temples by those holding the sealing powers of priesthood authority whereby that which is bound together on earth is also bound together in heaven.

Those couples so sealed together who remain true to their vows and are valiant in living the gospel will become, as the apostle Peter declared, "heirs together of the grace of life" (1 Peter 3:7), meaning that together, as husband and wife, they share in the gift of eternal life. For the Lord has made clear that "neither is the man without the woman, neither the woman without the man, in the Lord" (1 Corinthians 11:11).

Such a prospect may not sound overly exciting to someone on earth who is currently struggling in an unhappy marriage. But remember that the gospel of Jesus Christ was established to help people become perfect, even as their Father in Heaven is perfect. (See Matthew 5:48.) As a couple work together to make the gospel an integral part of their lives and begin the process of becoming truly kind, loving, unselfish, and Christlike individuals, they will find that the love they once shared for one another will come alive again. They will also learn that the greatest happiness they can experience in this life, as well as in the next life, will come mainly from the close marital and family relationships they have developed.

The Prophet Joseph also learned that the Lord has not forgotten those individuals who, through no fault of their own, do not receive the opportunity to be married in this life, or who have been divorced or "unequally yoked" (2 Corinthians 6:14) to a marriage partner who proves unworthy of a celestial inheritance. Such individuals, if they have lived worthy of this blessing and have a desire to do so, will receive the opportunity while in the spirit world to meet and be joined to an equally worthy partner— an eternal companion whom they will come to love. God is perfectly just and fair, and He will not deprive any of His children of blessings they have proven worthy and desirous to receive.

In the lower kingdoms of heaven, men and women have no such blessings offered. Their marriages upon the earth are quite literally "until death do us part." This should come as no surprise to us, for even while Christ was living in mortality He spoke of the temporary nature of marriage unions entered into by those without the gospel, declaring that in the next life these people "neither marry, nor are given in marriage, but are as the angels of God in heaven" (Matthew 22:30).

Having carefully and prayerfully studied the teachings of the Holy Bible and early Christian leaders on this subject—and then having compared these teachings with those revealed anew to the Prophet Joseph Smith—I know beyond a shadow of doubt that what Joseph saw and taught is true. Once again, unlike so many of the teachings of the modern Christian world, the teachings of *original* Christianity actually make sense. God really *is* perfectly just and fair in His judgments. What a tremendous blessing it is to have these pure teachings of Christ restored to earth and once again available to us.

Now, What Do You Believe?

If you were asked, how would you answer this question: Do those individuals who are basically good people, but who are lukewarm in their devotion to God, end up going to heaven or to hell? (Mentally, check one of these three answers.)

Modern: I agree with the teachings of many modern Christian churches that such individuals will go to heaven. As long as a person confesses a belief in Christ, that's all that really matters. What kind of life he or she actually lives—valiant or lukewarm—really has little or no bearing on the matter, since our good works and righteous deeds play no part in the attainment of salvation.

Modern: I agree with those many other modern Christian churches that teach that such an individual will go to hell. In the Bible, God says, "Because thou art lukewarm, and neither cold nor hot, I will spue thee out of my mouth" (Revelation 3:16). Those who are not fully committed and obedient to God do not go to heaven and therefore can only reside in hell.

Ancient and Restored: I agree with the teachings of *original* Christianity that because God is perfectly just and fair, He has provided an appropriate reward or punishment for each of His children. A basically good person who is lukewarm in His devotion to God will neither be sent to hell with the wicked nor sent to the highest of heavens to dwell with the Father. In His justice and mercy, these people will be rewarded for their goodness but will be denied far greater blessings that they could have received had they been more faithful in their commitment to Him.

Note 1: Among the many hundreds of religions and religious sects that exist upon the earth today, both Christian and non-Christian, it seems that most people believe that those belonging to their particular church or belief system will go to heaven to live with God while everyone else will ultimately either cease to exist or will dwell eternally in hell. Fortunately for us, God is far kinder and much more loving and merciful to His children than what most religious leaders and their followers believe.

The Prophet Joseph Smith learned that good and honorable people of all religious faiths, both Christian and non-Christian (and even those of no faith at all), will be rewarded for their goodness—for all men will be judged "according to their works" (Revelation 20:12–13). Of course, due to God's grace and perfect love towards His children, each will receive eternal blessings far, far greater and more glorious than anything they might have actually *earned* from performing a few good deeds during their short life on earth. Nevertheless, it is their righteous deeds and virtuous character that *qualify* them for such blessings. At the time of the final great judgment of mankind, all will come to know that Jesus is the Christ—for He is that great Judge before whom they will stand. (See Luke 7:24.) Those who never fully accepted Him or His true gospel while on earth or while dwelling in the spirit world, but nevertheless who have lived very good lives, will enter into a heavenly paradise or "second" heaven. Due to God's love and mercy, they will indeed receive that very heaven most of them have come to expect and look forward to.

In this paradise or heaven, they will not see or live in the presence of God the Father—but, of course, most people believe that the Father is a formless, invisible substance without substance that cannot actually be seen anyway. These people will occasionally be visited by the presence of Jesus Christ. (The Prophet Joseph Smith learned that the influence of the Holy Ghost presides over the first heaven, Jesus Christ the second heaven, and God the Father reigns supreme in the third or highest of heavens.) Those dwelling in the first paradise or heaven will not be married or live as families—but, of course, their churches have taught them that there is no marriage in heaven, and so most people do not expect this blessing anyway. Thus, in the mercy of God, most people will indeed receive the very heaven they have come to expect.

Christ's mission on earth, however, was not simply to save good and honorable people in paradise or the second heaven. A person does not initially even have to believe in Christ in order to qualify for this reward. Christ's mission was and still is to bring people back to the presence of His and our Father, there to enjoy the blessings of supreme happiness, exaltation, and eternal life in the third or highest of heavens.

Note 2: Having spent some time speaking of heaven, perhaps it might be of some worth to interject here just a few comments about hell—that place and state of mind where the unrepentant wicked will pay the required punishment for their sins.

The Prophet Joseph Smith learned that hell is much different than many suppose. Speaking figuratively, in the scriptures the apostle John very vividly and descriptively speaks of hell as "a lake of fire and brimstone" (Revelation 20:10) into which the wicked will be thrown at the time of death. Remarkably, many religious leaders even today take this description quite literally, supposing that God sends sinners off to be eternally, physically tortured in hellfire. Obviously, if this were true, God would rank greater in cruelty than a whole host of tyrants, madmen, and barbarians who over the history of this earth have delighted in the torture and murder of their opponents and victims. How silly and inconceivable to think that a God of perfect love could ever behave in such a manner! Those who believe or teach such nonsense obviously have no idea of the true nature of God.

The lake of fire and brimstone of which John speaks is symbolic of the terrible guilt, sorrow, and mental anguish that the unrepentant wicked will suffer for their sins. Today, while in mortality, many believe they can hide their sins and are able to rationalize away their evil deeds. Some have so hardened their consciences that they feel no guilt whatsoever for their wickedness. But such will not always be the case, for in the spirit world, those consigned to hell will vividly recall each evil act they have perpetrated. Figuratively speaking, their consciences will be seared as with a hot iron, and they will literally experience "weeping, wailing, and gnashing of teeth" (Matthew 13:42, 50; 22:13; 24:51).

The punishment that the wicked receive in hell is actually not administered by God (although, being a perfectly just God, He does allow and even require it to take place). Rather, it is a terrible mental and emotional punishment that the wicked inflict upon themselves and each other. God wants none of His children to experience this terrible suffering. This is why He has His prophets so vividly describe it, and why He forewarns His children concerning it. In truth, it breaks His heart that any of His children must endure and suffer such horrible punishment.

In the mercy of God, hell does not last forever. Could a God of love really allow His children to remain in such terrible anguish throughout all eternity, or to be punished far beyond that which they deserve? Christ was not required to spend an eternity of suffering in order to pay for the sins of those who repent, and neither does God require that an unrepentant man or woman spend an eternity of suffering to pay for their own sins. Once they have experienced sufficient suffering for their sins (which punishment will last for a minimum of one thousand years) and have learned obedience to those laws by which they are and will be subject, they will be brought out of hell to stand before the Savior to be judged. (See Revelation 20:13.)

At this time, the vast majority of those who have come out of hell will be resurrected with immortal, physical bodies comparable to the glory of the stars and will be admitted into the first and lowest heaven. This will indeed be a heaven where there will no longer be physical illness, suffering, wars, or evil and contention among men. But remember that the happiness they receive will only be comparable to the light and glory we can observe emitting from a star. Such a feeling of peace and happiness can scarcely compare to the light and glory coming from the moon, and pales when compared to the light and glory streaming from the sun.

Yes, because of God's loving and merciful nature, once they have sufficiently paid the price of justice, these souls will receive neither a beautiful paradise nor a truly magnificent life of royalty in God's presence, but nevertheless it is a peaceful, heaven-like abode. Imagine, however, the deep regret a person will feel knowing he could have received such an infinitely greater reward and degree of happiness through all eternity had he been obedient to God's commandments during the great test of mortality.

Our spirits are sent to earth for basically two purposes: (1) to have the opportunity to obtain a physical body, and (2) to be tested. While living on earth and in the spirit world, God is closely watching us. He is observing our true nature and character in action. We are all given the chance and are free to accept the truth, to repent of our sins, and to obtain divine forgiveness. Sadly, however, most of God's children will reject the truth, and many will regularly choose to do evil over good. Oh, so many individuals miserably fail the test that they were sent to earth to participate in.

Although required to temporarily suffer great mental and emotional anguish in hell, God's eternal punishment to the wicked is more aptly described as a withholding of those far greater blessings that could have been obtained throughout all eternity if the wicked had but lived worthy to receive them.

NOTES

1. Saint Irenaeus, *Against Heresies*, iv, 27, quoted in James L. Barker, *Apostasy from the Divine Church* (Salt Lake City: Bookcraft, 1984), 63.
2. Justin Martyr, *Dialogue with Trypo*, lxxii, 4, quoted in Barker, *Apostasy*, 63.
3. Shepherd of Hermas, Sim., ix, xvi, 5, quoted in Barker, *Apostasy*, 63.
4. Lake, footnote 1, in his translation of *The Shepherd in Apostolic Fathers*, vol. 2, 263, The Loeb Classical Library, quoted in Barker, *Apostasy*, 63.

5. The position of the Roman Catholic Church was changed from exclusivism to the more liberal teaching of inclusivism at the last ecumenical council, Vatican II, held at Rome in 1960.

6. Saint Irenaeus, *Against Heresies*, vol. 2, quoted in Barker, *Apostasy*; italics added.

7. Clement of Alexandria, in Tixeront, *Histoire des Dogmes*, vol. 1, 296, quoted in Barker, *Apostasy*, 69.

8. LeGrand Richards, *A Marvelous Work and a Wonder* (Salt Lake City: Deseret Book, 2004), 253.

SECTION II
THE GREAT APOSTASY

Question #3

Why are there so many different Christian churches upon the earth today?

The Savior Himself revealed to the Prophet Joseph Smith that there had been a great apostasy or falling away from the truths of His pure gospel during the Middle and Dark Ages. It did not take a direct revelation from God, however, for other thinking men to come to this same conclusion. For example, Thomas Jefferson, one of America's great founding fathers and a sincere believer in God, would never join any Christian church during his lifetime. Why not? In speaking of Christianity as it existed in his day (the early nineteenth century), Jefferson declared,

> The religion builders have so distorted and deformed the doctrines of Jesus, so muffled them in mysticisms, fancies, and falsehoods, have caricatured them into forms so inconceivable, as to shock reasonable thinkers. . . . Happy in the prospect of a restoration of primitive Christianity, I must leave to younger persons to encounter and lop off the false branches which have been engrafted into it by the mythologists of the middle and modern ages.[1]

In Jefferson's day, as in our own, many different Christian churches existed, each possessing beliefs and doctrines that so often contradicted the teachings of other Christian sects. Jefferson believed the reason that so much confusion, contention, and division existed within the modern Christian world was simply because Christian churches no longer taught the original teachings of Christ.

Perhaps a very brief explanation of how this apostasy, or falling away from truth, took place in ancient times will help you to understand why Jefferson, and so many others of his day, chose to join none of the current churches.

The Apostasy

When Jesus Christ was upon the earth, He declared, "I will build my church" (Matthew 16:18). This church, as He indicated, was indeed *His* church—The Church of Jesus Christ. During the earliest years of the Christian era, all baptized members of His church were called Saints. From among those who followed the Savior, He chose twelve men. Upon these men He laid His hands, and they were ordained apostles, their mission being to act as special witnesses of His divine nature and mission.

In the Lord's Church, true doctrines leading to salvation were taught in simplicity and clarity. After Christ's departure, men holding valid priesthood authority from God led the Church through continuing divine revelation. As long as this communication between Christ and His leaders continued, the Church would never stray from the truth.

The early apostles were responsible for administering the affairs of the Church, including preaching the true gospel and calling and ordaining local Church officers and leaders. They also made certain that the Church remained pure and untainted by any rituals or philosophies taken from the contemporary pagan religions of the day. For as the apostle Paul declared, "What fellowship hath righteousness with unrighteousness? and what communion hath light with darkness? And what concord hath Christ with Belial [a pagan god]? or what part hath he that believeth with an infidel? And what agreement hath the temple of God with idols? . . . Wherefore come out from among them, and be ye separate, saith the Lord, and touch not the unclean thing" (2 Corinthians 6:14–17).

In spite of the Lord's admonition to "touch not" the unclean things of paganism, later Church leaders proved all too anxious to do just that. As centuries passed, many new converts to the Church, from pagan backgrounds, were dissatisfied with the simplicity of Christian worship and its lack of pomp and ritual. To appease these converts and, at the same time, to make the Church more appealing to potential converts, Church leaders began to introduce pagan mysticism and rites into the worship services. Describing the condition of the Church during the fourth century, Dr. J. L. von Mosheim, religious historian and chancellor of the University of Gottingen (AD 1755) wrote,

The Christian bishops introduced, with but slight alterations, into

Christian worship, those rites and institutions by which the Greeks and Romans and other nations had manifested their piety and reverence towards their imaginary deities. The bishops supposed that the people would more readily embrace Christianity if they saw that the rites handed down to them from their fathers still existed unchanged among the Christians. These new converts perceived that Christ and the martyrs were worshipped in the same manner as their gods had been. There was, of course, little difference, in these times, between the public worship of the Christians and that of the Greeks and Romans. In both alike, there were splendid robes, mitres (tall, ornate hats worn by the priests), tiaras, wax tapers, crosiers, processions, illustrations, statues and other icons before which the people knelt and worshipped, golden and silver vases, and numberless other things.[2]

While the apostle Paul had counseled members of the Church that they remove themselves from and stay untainted by the practice of infidels, idol worshippers, and followers of the pagan god Belial; history makes clear that the people and their leaders were quick to embrace those very practices the Lord had strictly forbidden. It proved much easier to lower the standards of Christianity to conform to the pagan practices of the people than to lift the people to conform to the high standards of Christianity.

In attempting to justify this marriage of Christianity and heathendom, however, no less an authority than the highly-respected Roman Catholic cardinal of Great Britain, John Henry Newman in the nineteenth century, wrote,

> (Section 1 and 2) Confiding then in the power of Christianity to resist the infection of evil, and *to transmute the very instruments and appendages of demon-worship* [i.e. satanic rituals] *to an evangelical use*, and feeling also that these usages had originally come from primitive revelations and from the instinct of nature, though they had been corrupted; and that they must invent what they needed, if they did not use what they found; and that they were moreover possessed of the very archetypes of which *paganism* attempted the shadows; *the rulers of the Church from early times were prepared, should the occasion arise, to adopt, or imitate, or sanction the existing rites and customs of the [pagan] populace, as well as the philosophy of the educated class* [i.e., the teachings of the ancient Greek philosophers, Plato and Aristotle].
>
> The use of temples and these dedicated to particular saints, and ornamented on occasion with the branches of trees; incense lamps, and candles; votive offerings on recovery from illness; holy water; asylums,

holydays, and seasons, use of calendars, processions, blessings on the fields, sacerdotal vestments [magnificent robes worn by the clergy], the tonsure, the ring in marriage, turning to the East, images [bowing before statues], perhaps the ecclesiastical chant, and the Kyrie Eleison (the petition "Lord have mercy on us"), *are all of pagan origin*, and sanctified by their adoption into the Church.[3]

Cardinal Newman, as well as millions of other modern Christians, can see little or no harm in worshipping God in the same manner that ancient pagans worshipped their imaginary gods. Yet one is forced to wonder just how our Heavenly Father might view such pomp, ritual, and false philosophies, all invented by man, which are so obviously in direct conflict with His original, divinely revealed instructions to His children.

During the earliest years of Christianity, the pure doctrines of Christ had been given to Church leaders through direct revelation from heaven. There was no room for debate or any question about the truth and purity of these teachings. As centuries passed, however, and Christianity became more and more engulfed in pagan ritual and philosophy, the heavens began to close and eventually revelation to the Church completely ceased. With no apostles, prophets, or divinely-appointed Church leaders, soon numberless councils arose, often for the purpose of debating Church doctrine or practice. At these councils, many of the teachings of the early Church were rejected or lost; other original teachings were greatly modified; and new teachings, totally outside the realm of scripture or the early revelations, were added to the doctrines of the Church.

During the Middle Ages, while the clergy was forever engaging in heated debate over the meaning of the scriptures and in the formulation of new doctrines and creeds, laymembers of the Church were strictly forbidden to read from the Bible. Religious leaders determined that maintaining unity in the Church could only be accomplished by keeping the people as ignorant of the canon of scripture as possible. With the invention of the printing press in Europe, however, copies of the Bible became readily available to many laymembers of the Church. Just as Church leaders had feared, when people began to actually read from the Bible itself, many recognized that the Church had strayed far from its original moorings.

Those who dared to voice their objections or opinions concerning Church doctrine or practice, or who chose to break away from the Church of Rome, were labeled as heretics. Tens of thousands of these dissenters were imprisoned, tortured, or killed. Even the fear of imprisonment, torture, and death could not greatly slow the movement, however, and as the rebellion against the teachings of Rome continued to spread, the so-called heretics grew in number much faster than the Roman Catholic Church was able to put them to death. Thus we find the first Protestant churches coming into existence.

Two of the most prominent Protestant leaders, Martin Luther of Germany and Ulrich Zwingli of Switzerland, met together in hopes of forming a new church. In their discussions they found, however, that they could not agree on the meaning of various passages of scripture contained in the Bible. Unable to reconcile their differences, they parted and formed two separate new churches—the Lutheran and the Reformed (Presbyterian).

As many other reformers observed the teachings of these two churches, however, they determined that both of these also had errors in their interpretation of the scriptures. So these individuals decided to form their own churches, like Luther and Zwingli had done previously. As this process continued, dozens of new churches suddenly sprang into existence.

Eventually the number of new sects being formed would number in the hundreds, the leaders of each of these churches putting forth their own interpretation of the Bible. As a result, each church had its own unique set of doctrines and practices. Of course, the founders of each church believed that they understood the *true* meaning of the scriptures, far more so than the leaders of any other church. In truth, however, with the heavens closed and the benefit of direct revelation from God no longer available to guide them (as they readily admitted was the case), the best these religious leaders could do was to put forth their own best educated guess at what the scriptures were teaching. And—as badly splintered modern Christendom readily attests—one man's guess was, more often than not, much different from another man's.

Thus, what a state of confusion we have in Christianity today! For example, one modern Christian church will teach that baptism by water is necessary for salvation, while another will say it isn't. Some churches baptize infants; others say that a person must first have faith in Jesus Christ before being baptized. One church teaches that Satan is a literal being; another says that he is simply a figurative representation of evil. One church teaches that men and women are predestined for either heaven or hell before they are even born; another says that God gives us freedom to choose good or evil and our choices will determine our eternal destiny. Some churches teach that our eternal reward is based upon our good works, while others say that we are saved by grace alone and that good works are not required for salvation. For just about any specific doctrine that a modern Christian church teaches, we can find another church teaching just the opposite.

Some will say that all of these differences in doctrines and beliefs really don't matter. But what if, for example, baptism by water really is necessary for salvation, and your particular church teaches that it isn't? Is there safety in belonging to a church in which perhaps half its teachings are somewhat or basically true, but half or more are also totally false?

Many of these new Protestant churches chose to eliminate the magnificent clerical robes and some of the other outward manifestations and imitations of pagan worship that had entered the Roman Church through the centuries. However, as we will soon discuss more fully, none of these new sects were able to cast aside the influence of ancient Greek philosophy that had become so totally intertwined in the teachings of the medieval Church.

Thus was the state of religious affairs at the beginning of the nineteenth century. Greatly influenced by both pagan rites and heathen philosophies, and subject to countless personal, uninspired interpretations of scripture by men, Christianity had splintered into scores of different sects and had become what Thomas Jefferson would describe as a mass of "distorted and deformed" doctrines, totally engulfed in "mysticisms, fancies, and falsehoods" that would "shock" anyone of a reasonable mind.

QUESTION #4

Why do Mormons call themselves Latter-day Saints? Do they think that they are perfect or better than other people?

ORIGINAL CHRISTIAN TEACHINGS

During the early years of the Christian era, all those who had become associated with the Church of Jesus Christ by receiving the ordinance of baptism were called Saints. Speaking to some newly converted members of the Church at Ephesus, the apostle Paul declared, "Now therefore ye are no more strangers and foreigners, but *fellowcitizens with the saints*, and of the household of God" (Ephesians 2:19; italics added).

Throughout the pages of the New Testament, members of the Church are constantly referred to by this title. As modern religious scholars note, "in the New Testament the 'saints' are all those who by baptism have entered into the Christian covenant (see Acts 9:13, 32, 41; Romans 1:7; 1 Cor. 1:2; Phil. 1:1). The use of the title does not assert the existence of high moral qualities, but implies them as a duty (1 Peter 1:14, 15)."[4]

The scriptures teach us that the Lord established His church "for the perfecting of the saints" (Ephesians 4:12), that is, to help its imperfect members (Saints) to become perfect even as He is perfect.

As part of the latter-day restoration of original Christian teachings and practices to the earth, members of the Lord's modern church are once again called Saints, just as they were during the days of the early apostles. As Latter-day Saints, we certainly do not consider ourselves to be perfect or in any way above or superior to other people, although we have made a covenant to try to follow the teachings of the Savior to the best of our abilities. The confusion regarding this matter is due to the change in the meaning of the title, Saint, that took place within Christianity during medieval times.

MEDIEVAL AND MODERN CHRISTIAN TEACHINGS

Recalling Cardinal Newman's statement that during the Middle Ages Church leaders were well "prepared . . . to adopt, or imitate, or sanction"[5] the existing rites and practices of the pagan world, not many years after the passing of the apostles, the use of the term *Saint* was completely changed. Rather than continue to apply to all baptized members of the Church, now in imitation of the reverence given to deified heroes and to multiple gods by the pagan world, the term became restricted to refer only to certain individuals who had lived unusually holy and pure lives, or who had died as martyrs in the cause of Christ. At first the local bishops determined who were to be canonized as Saints; but this later became the sole prerogative of the bishop of Rome, also known as the Pope.

As centuries passed, many practices borrowed from paganism began to be associated with the veneration or worship of these saints and martyrs, such as that of making pilgrimages to the tombs of dead saints. In imitation of how the heathen world worshipped its many heroes and gods, Christian men and women would often travel hundreds of miles to worship at temples, shrines, or tombs that had been dedicated to honor saints. By showing such devotion, it was hoped that the particular saint being so honored would have compassion upon the sinner and plead his case before God.

Over time, other pagan practices also became associated with the outright worship of saints.

Early Church leaders had criticized the worship of images and idols by the pagan world. Following the scriptural teachings of the apostle Paul, early Church councils had condemned such heathen practices, forbidding them within the Church. However, by late in the fourth century Christians had begun the practice of bowing and worshipping before pictures, and still later before statues that had been created in a saint's image.

> The wit of the Christian apologists [early Church writers who wrote in defense of Christian teachings] was pointed against the foolish idolaters, who bowed before the workmanship of their own hands . . . the first notice of the use of pictures [in the Church] is in the censure of the council of Illiberis, three hundred years after the Christian era. . . . At first, the experiment was made with caution and scruple; and the venerable pictures were discreetly allowed to instruct the ignorant, to awaken the cold, and to gratify the prejudices of the heathen proselytes. By a slow though inevitable progression, the honors of the original were transferred to the copy; the devout Christian prayed before the image of a saint; and the Pagan rites of genuflection [bowing], luminaries [candles], and incense again stole into the Catholic church. . . . The use, and even the worship, of images was firmly established before the end of the sixth century.[6]

During the time of Augustine (AD 354–430) no statues yet existed; however, he reluctantly admitted that in his day there were many "adorers of pictures."[7] As the Protestant religious historian Philip Schaff records, "A superstitious fancy even invented stories of wonder-working pictures, and ascribed to them motion, speech, and action."[8]

Eventually the veneretion and worship of pictures gave way to similar reverence towards statues. It is most remarkable, of course, that Church leaders could rationalize the practice of actually bowing before "graven images" when it was in direct opposition to the second of the Ten Commandments, which had been so clearly and forcefully stated by God and recorded in the Bible. (See Exodus 20:4–6.)

While the veneration, and in some cases actual worship of pictures, statues, and other icons or images was for many centuries a subject of great controversy, the worship "of the saints was everywhere popular. New feasts were established in their honor. . . . Their remains, or even fragments of them, were everywhere in great demand, and though at first their relics were religiously preserved in the churches, it soon became customary to carry them about in processions, to bear them in battle, and to dispose of them in exchange for alms destined for building of churches."[9]

According to Robertson, "The digging up and dismembering of the bodies of saints had become so prevalent by the first half of the 4th century (356), that St. Anthony, after giving away his fewer than half dozen belongings, charged his disciples that on his death they bury him in a place unknown to any but themselves, 'lest his remains . . . be embalmed and kept above ground' (Robertson, *History of the Christian Church*, II, 6, 61)."[10]

Because of the multiplicity of counterfeit relics that existed, "Theodosius enacted (in 386) a law forbidding the buying and selling of the bodies of martyrs, or the moving of them from one place to another."[11]

J. Reuben Clark Jr. quotes various historians who further discuss this most remarkable belief in the divine powers of relics: "The Bishop of Hippo, who felt that Hippo had been less favorably treated than other places, recorded some seventy miracles, including three resurrections from the dead, wrought in two years by the relics he had, but he wanted more."[12]

> But the law of Theodosius above noted, neither cured nor . . . curbed the credulity of the people nor the cupidity of fakirs. Relics multiplied in unbelievable numbers and of impossible objects.
>
> In England at Walsingham, Erasmus (1466–1536) was shown the Virgin's congealed milk and the middle joint of one of Peter's fingers. At Cantebury, Erasmus and Colet were shown relics of Thomas Becket, including the "rags with which the archbishop had blown his nose. Colet held them only a moment in his fingers and let them drop in disgust" (Schaff, *History of the Christian Church*, 742).
>
> In Germany, the friars purveyed all sorts of merchandise "from the bones of Balaam's ass to the straw of the manger and feathers from St. Michael's wings" (Schaff, *History of the Christian Church*, 742).
>
> In Vienna, they displayed a piece of Noah's ark, drops of the sweat of Jesus in the Garden of Gethsamane, as well as some of the incense brought to the Christ child by Wise Men from the East (Schaff, *History of the Christian Church*, 742).[13]

It was commonly believed that these relics possessed supernatural powers. At the seventh General Council (AD 787), held at Nicea, it was declared that no new church edifice could be erected without a relic (a bone or other sacred artifact) to reside within it. Even in the supposedly more enlightened days of the Renaissance (sixteenth century),

> Princes rivaled each other in collecting the relics of saints. . . . In the time of Luther, Frederick the Wise . . . had accumulated no less than five thousand of the sacred objects. In a catalogue of them, we find the rod of Moses, a bit of the burning bush, thread spun by the virgin,

etc. The elector of Mayence possessed even a larger collection, which included forty-two whole bodies of saints and some earth from a field near Damascus out of which God was supposed to have created man.[14]

John Calvin, the well-known Protestant reformer, wrote a tract concerning the superstitious heathen practice (later embraced by Christianity) of collecting, displaying, and actually worshipping relics, and commented upon some of the more famous and popular relics that existed in the Roman Church during his own day (sixteenth century). The historian Schaff both quotes and comments upon Calvin's writings as follows:

> What was at first a foolish curiosity for preserving relics has degenerated into abominable idolatry. The great majority of the relics are spurious. It could be shown by comparison that every apostle has more than four bodies and every saint two or three. The arm of St. Anthony, which was worshipped in Geneva [Switzerland], when brought out of the case, turned out to be part of a stag. The body of Christ could not be obtained, but the monks of Charroux pretend to have, besides teeth and hair, the prepuce or pellicle cut off in his circumcision. But it is shown also in the Lateran church at Rome.
>
> Fragments of the cross . . . are scattered over many churches in Italy, France, Spain, etc., and would form a good shipload, which it would take three hundred men to carry instead of one. But they say that this wood never grows less! Some affirm that their fragments were carried by angels, others that they dropped down from heaven. . . . There is still greater controversy as to the three nails of the cross: one of them was fixed in the crown of Constantine, the other two were fitted to his horse's bridle, according to Theodoret, or one was kept by Helena herself, according to Ambrose. But now there are two nails at Rome, one at Siena, . . . one at Cologne, one at Treves, two at Paris, one at Bourges, etc. All of the claims are equally good, for the nails are all spurious. There is also more than one soldier's spear, crown of thorns, purple robe, the seamless coat, and Veronica's napkin (which at least six cities boast of having). A piece of broiled fish, which Peter offered to the risen Lord on the seashore, must have been wondrously well salted if it has kept for these fifteen centuries! But, jesting apart, is it supposable that the apostles made relics of what they had actually prepared for dinner?
>
> Calvin exposes with equal effect the absurdities and impieties of the wonder-working pictures of Christ; the relics of the hair and milk of the Virgin Mary, preserved in so many places, her combs, her wardrobe and baggage, and her house carried by angels across the sea

to Loreto; the shoes of St. Joseph; the slippers of St. James; the head of John the Baptist, of which Rhodes, Malta, Lucca, Nevers, Amiens, Besancon, and Noyan claim to have portions; and his fingers, one of which is shown at Besancon, another at Toulouse, another at Lyons, another at Bourges, another at Florence. At Avignon they have the sword with which John was beheaded, at Aix-la-Chapelle the linen cloth placed under him by the kindness of the executioner, in Rome his girdle and the altar at which he said prayers in the desert. It is strange, adds Calvin, that they do not also make him perform mass.

The tract concludes with this remark: "So completely are the relics mixed up and huddled together, that it is impossible to have the bones of any martyr without running the risk of worshipping the bones of some thief or robber, or, it may be, the bones of a dog, or a horse, or an ass, or—Let every one, therefore, guard against this risk. Henceforth, no man will be able to excuse himself by pretending ignorance."[15]

It is obvious to see that during the Middle and Dark Ages a great apostasy from true Christian teachings had occurred. The superstitions of paganism had become deeply entrenched within the Church, and along with so many other original Christian doctrines and practices, had totally replaced early Christian teachings concerning "the Saints."

CHRIST'S ORIGINAL TEACHINGS RESTORED TO JOSEPH SMITH

As we previously noted, in the Lord's original, true Church *all* baptized members were called Saints. There was no pagan-derived, superstitious worship of pictures, statues, bones, or other relics of the dead.

In speaking of names and titles, besides having members who were called Saints, if Christ's original, true Church were still upon the earth today, I would expect this Church to have actually been founded by Christ Himself and to be named after Him. For the Savior, while living in mortality, had declared, "I will build *my* church" (Matthew 16:18; italics added). Indeed, this was His Church, even the Church of Jesus Christ that He had established. This Church was of divine origin, having been founded by the Savior Himself, not by a man, woman, or group of individuals who had merely been studying the Bible and giving the world their new interpretation of it.

Today we often see churches that bear the names of the men who founded them. Some bear the name of a particular type of organization or government under which they function. Others bear the name of the country in which they were established, or the name of a particular doctrine or practice emphasized by or unique to their particular sect. But certainly, would not the Lord's Church, if it truly were His, have *both* been founded by Him and bear His name?

It is thus interesting to note that in 1830—the year in which Joseph Smith, acting under the direction of the Savior, reestablished Christ's original Church upon the earth—there was not a major church organization then existing upon the earth that actually bore the Savior's name. Although a few have copied this pattern since that time, none of these modern churches are patterned after His original church or claim to have been established by Him.

It is my witness to you, dear reader, that even as it existed anciently, the Church of Jesus Christ is once again upon the earth. The phrase "of Latter-day Saints" was added to the name of the Lord's modern-day church in order to distinguish it from the ancient Church of Jesus Christ and its members (Saints). All of the Saints, both ancient and modern, are members of the same church, just living in different time periods of the earth's history.

How fortunate we are to have early Christian teachings restored again to earth. What a blessing that we no longer need to be "strangers and foreigners" to truth, but can once again be "fellowcitizens with the saints, and of the household of God" (Ephesians 2:19).

QUESTION #5

At church I was taught that Adam and Eve were the first parents of the human family, and that Adam's transgression in the Garden of Eden was a terrible tragedy, bringing about mankind's fallen, mortal state. I was further told that all people are held personally accountable for Adam's original sin. If this is true, will my infant daughter, who died in my arms just moments after her birth, before I could have the stains of original sin removed through baptism, be unworthy to enter God's presence and thus be damned for all eternity?

ORIGINAL CHRISTIAN TEACHINGS

In the early years of Christianity, it was taught that the transgression of Adam and Eve in the Garden of Eden (eating the forbidden fruit) brought upon them—and upon all of mankind after them—physical death, or the ability to physically die. This transgression caused a physical change to take place in the bodies of our first parents, changing them from immortal to mortal beings. This act also brought upon them a spiritual death—that is, a loss of the blessing of having God's spirit with them, and of being allowed to actually stand in His divine presence and to talk directly to Him as they had previously done while living in the garden. (See Genesis 3.) In order to overcome the effects of these two deaths, God provided a Savior to redeem fallen man.

Because Jesus Christ was born of a mortal mother, Mary, He had the ability to physically die. Because He had an immortal Father, He also possessed the ability to overcome physical death and to take up His life again. When the Savior rose from the tomb on that first Easter morning, He forever broke the bonds of physical death. This made it possible for *all* men and women to eventually rise from the dead and enjoy the blessings of the resurrection, which is a reuniting of our physical body with our spirit body. Thus, through Christ, physical death has no hold over mankind. As the apostle Paul declared, "For since by man [Adam] came death, by man [Christ] came also the resurrection of the dead. For as in Adam *all* die, even so in Christ shall *all* be made alive" (1 Corinthians 15:21–22; italics added).

The resurrection is a free gift given to *all* mankind simply due to the love or grace of God towards His children.

Christ also made it possible for men and women to overcome spiritual death. As individuals exercise faith in the Savior and humbly repent of their transgressions, the Savior forgives them and removes their sins. He can do this because He has already personally suffered the punishment that, in the justice of God, is required for their sins. Of course, if a man does not exercise faith in the Savior and humbly request forgiveness of his sins, then, in the justice of God, he will remain spiritually dead and ultimately will be required to suffer the punishment due for his own sins. Thus, how important it is for each of us to look to the Savior in order to avoid and overcome spiritual suffering and death.

Through Christ's Atonement for sin and the principle of repentance, the stains of sin can be removed. A person can be pronounced clean—and therefore worthy—to enjoy the blessing of God's spirit dwelling within him while on earth, as well as the blessing of one day living in His actual presence. But in order for Christ's sacrifice for sin to take effect in our lives, the Savior taught that each of us must strive to become humble, innocent, and pure, even "as a little child" (Mark 10:13–16), or we cannot enter the kingdom of God.

MEDIEVAL AND MODERN CHRISTIAN TEACHINGS

In approximately AD 400, a north-African bishop by the name of

Augustine speculated that at the time of Adam's fall, not only did both physical death and spiritual death enter the world, but simultaneously all men inherited the stains of Adam's so-called original sin. (This phrase originated with Augustine and is not found in the Bible.) The corrupting effect of this sin could only be removed by baptism. According to Augustine, a tiny infant dying without baptism, although obviously possessing no personal sins, was nevertheless stained by original sin and was therefore doomed to an eternity of physical suffering in hellfire.

This doctrine of Augustine, being new to Christianity and without any scriptural support to justify it, was heatedly debated among the clergy for the next hundred years. The eastern or Greek-speaking portion of the medieval Church (from which sprang the Greek Orthodox, Russian Orthodox, Armenian Orthodox, and other churches) ultimately rejected this doctrine, declaring it to be merely a human invention. In this regard, as one western, Protestant religious historian would admit, "the Augustinian system was unknown in the ante-Nicene age [prior to AD 325], and was never accepted in the Eastern church. This is a strong historical argument against it."[16]

In spite of the fact that this doctrine was not supported by the scriptures, was never taught within the Church during the first four centuries of the Christian era, and was totally rejected by the eastern half of the Church, nevertheless most of the western or Latin-speaking part of the Church (from which sprang the Roman Catholic and later the Protestant sects) did eventually accept it. The West's acceptance of this doctrine was due in large part to the fact that it finally provided some support and justification for the doctrine of infant baptism—the first isolated instances of this practice appearing within the Church less than one hundred years after the removal of the last living apostle, John the Beloved, from the active ministry.

Similar to the doctrine of original sin, the doctrine of infant baptism is not taught in the scriptures, and there is absolutely no evidence that it was ever practiced during the early years of Christianity. As noted by the well-known reformer Martin Luther himself, "It cannot be proven by the sacred scriptures that infant baptism was instituted by Christ, or begun by the first Christians after the apostles."[17]

The New Testament indicates that early Jewish converts to the Church wanted to bring the ordinance of infant circumcision into Christianity. This practice (which was a part of the lesser law or law of Moses practiced by the Jews, and which Christ's higher law or gospel replaced) was forcefully denounced and prohibited in the scriptures by the apostle Paul in his epistles to the various branches of the early Church. A little more than a century later, however, after the death of the apostles and when they were no longer restrained by apostolic opposition, converts were able to introduce infant baptism into the Church as a substitute for Jewish infant circumcision. While the scriptures taught that an individual must first have faith in Christ, repent of his sins, and then signify his acceptance of Christ as his Savior through entering the waters of baptism, this procedure was now completely reversed in that an infant was first baptized and then years later would be taught to believe in Christ.

By Augustine's day, infant baptism had become common but was far from universally practiced. After his doctrine of original sin was completely accepted by the western Church (approximately AD 500), however, we see infant baptism being practiced everywhere, as parents were taught the quite terrifying doctrine that their tiny babies would suffer physical pain in an endless hell if they died without having original sin removed from them through baptism.

Even though the doctrine of original sin had become well-established and accepted in the western Church, it was still difficult for many to reconcile the belief in a just, loving, and merciful Christ, as taught in the scriptures, with a Being who would mercilessly send helpless little babies down to hell, there to burn for eternity. During the Middle Ages, this subject was one of great controversy and debate among the clergy. Some proposed that perhaps there was an intermediary state of existence between heaven and hell to which unbaptized babies were sent. Although unworthy to enter God's actual presence, there they could at least live for all eternity feeling neither suffering nor joy. The proponents of this doctrine named this place, or state of existence, limbo.

As the centuries passed and this doctrine continued to evolve and change, an even more popular theory came into existence. In an effort to overcome the obvious contradiction of a loving Christ sending babies off to eternally suffer in hell, during the thirteenth century Thomas Aquinas (AD 1227–1274) developed a new doctrine that unbaptized babies dwelling in limbo, although unworthy to be admitted into God's presence in heaven, actually lived in a state of eternal bliss and happiness.

This was a classic example of one erroneous teaching begetting another. Once one false practice (infant baptism) entered the Church, it required yet another human invention (original sin) to justify it. But these errors obviously created an inconsistency in doctrine (a loving God mercilessly sending helpless babies to hell), which would then require church leaders to invent still another new doctrine (limbo) to make some sense out of the earlier errors . . . and on and on it went.

Of course, with no divine revelation to guide them, all of the arguments and new doctrines these medieval church leaders invented were simply bogus—speculative theories that more often than not were far removed from the truth.

Centuries later, Protestant reformers recognized that the term *limbo* and the teaching that unbaptized infants resided in such a place were not found in the scriptures, nor was such a blissful abode found anywhere in Church doctrine for the first twelve hundred years of the Christian era. They rejected this doctrine as strictly a human invention, but meanwhile most retained a belief in original sin and infant baptism, many returning to the Puritanical view of infant damnation.

Without question, there are no teachings of apostate modern Christianity that are more unreasonable or more untrue than are these. As one modern critic of these radically perverted teachings notes,

> Few heresies have been more firmly lodged in the minds of large segments of fallen man than that of infant baptism. Some even say that because original sin begins not at birth but at conception itself, baptism is required not only for every aborted fetus, but even for a blood clot that has yet to take upon itself embryonic form. The traditional sectarian phrase in many of the sermons of the past was that the road to hell was paved with the skulls of unbaptized infants not a span [hand's width] long.[18]

One can but imagine what God must think of these doctrines as He sees Himself being portrayed as little more than a merciless barbarian. How very tragic that these false teachings and corrupt practices have been embraced by so many modern Christian churches. Just imagine—teaching that an infant that takes merely one breath in mortality and then quickly dies is immediately sent off by God to be forever tortured in hellfire. How could any reasonable person believe such a thing? How could anyone love and admire such a merciless Being or actually desire to be in the presence of a God who thinks nothing of torturing tiny babies? It simply defies comprehension.

CHRIST'S ORIGINAL TEACHINGS RESTORED TO JOSEPH SMITH

To the Prophet Joseph Smith, God revealed the truth that although the fall of Adam did bring both physical and spiritual deaths into the world, through Christ both of these obstacles to man's progression have been overcome. Through Christ, all men will overcome physical death through the blessings of the resurrection; and as a man develops faith in Christ, accepts His true gospel, sincerely repents of his sins, and is baptized, sin and spiritual death are also removed from him. A child comes into this world innocent, and thus in no need of baptism. Unless we ourselves become pure like a little child, we will not enter God's presence.

Try to imagine a doctrine more unreasonable than that of a perfectly just and loving God sending helpless little babies off to an endless hell, requiring them to be physically tortured for all eternity because they are stained by a sin that was committed by someone else—a sin for which they are totally incapable of repenting. Little wonder that my grandpa had great difficulty accepting such a doctrine. The Lord revealed to the Prophet Joseph Smith that this man-made teaching of modern Christendom is quite literally an abomination in His sight.

In the New Testament we read of Christ instructing His disciples to allow the little children to come to Him so that He might lay His hands on them and bless them—for the Savior loved these little ones so very much. The Lord's feelings about little children are no different today. In restoring His Church once again to the earth, the Lord instructed the Prophet Joseph Smith that little children were to be taken up in the arms of the members of the priesthood and given special blessings. They were not to be baptized until they had reached an age of sufficient maturity and understanding to be accountable before God for their actions. When they were capable of exercising a simple faith in Christ and of repenting of their sins, then they were to be baptized.

The gospel of Jesus Christ is beautifully simple and simply beautiful. It only ceases to make sense when men begin to change it. How blessed we are to have the pure gospel of Christ once more available to us.

The phrase "in whom all have sinned" was interpreted by Augustine to mean that the sin of Adam was passed down upon all of mankind—that God holds all men responsible for Adam's sin. The Latin Vulgate was a translation by Jerome from an earlier Greek version of the Bible. Catholic and Protestant scholars today admit that this was an incorrect translation of the verse. While the King James Version more accurately translates the phrase as "for that all have sinned," modern scholars agree that this phrase should actually be translated "because all have sinned."

Several modern scholars have commented on this verse:

> Saint Augustine attaches great importance to the celebrated passage of Saint Paul, Romans 5:12, and following; it is fitting to note that the words of the Greek text *eph' O pantes emarton*, on which he lays much stress, are badly translated in the Latin Vulgate by *in quo onmes peccaverunt*, and do not mean "in whom all have sinned," but "because all have sinned."[19]

> *In quo onmes peccaverunt:* this formula of the Vulgate should be translated: because all have sinned, *in quo* being understood in the sense *in eo quod (eph' O)*: all interpreters [translators] are in agreement on this point.[20]

> The exegesis of Augustine, and his doctrine of a personal fall, as it were of all men in Adam, are therefore doubtless untenable.[21]

The only scripture in the entire Bible by which Augustine was able to justify his new doctrine of original sin is recognized today by scholars of all faiths as a mistranslated verse from the Latin Vulgate. One can search the Bible from cover to cover and never find any verse that supports such a belief. Indeed, this doctrine fails the test of scripture; it fails the test of history; and it most certainly fails the test of logic and reason.

To their credit, most Protestant churches today have seen some of the folly and inconsistency of this doctrine that obviously portrays God as a merciless beast. Today, many religious leaders simply profess ignorance, not knowing what actually happens to unbaptized babies who die. Many others have rejected altogether the idea of infant damnation—a doctrine that was commonly and very forcefully taught in many of their churches just a century ago. Following a church study on the subject, in the year 2007 even the Pope himself publicly suggested that unbaptized infants who die might actually be allowed into heaven, admitting that the long-held doctrine of limbo may not be true at all. Meanwhile, the majority of these various churches continue to teach the doctrine of original sin and to practice infant baptism. And for what purpose do they baptize these infants? If, as they now profess, a child can die without baptism and still be saved in heaven, then why were they baptized in the first place? Obviously such an ordinance is meaningless to the tiny infant himself and, now, apparently meaningless to God as well. No matter how they try to correct some of these unreasonable and false doctrines of ages past, the many false doctrines and practices that remain (such as original sin and infant baptism) continue to defy any semblance of reason.

Now, What Do You Believe?

If a tiny baby dies before having the stains of original sin removed through baptism, will he or she be unclean and unworthy to enter God's presence, and thus be damned for all eternity? (Mentally, check one of these answers.)

Modern: I agree with the teachings of the largest modern Christian church that such infants are not worthy to enter God's presence and thus will never see Christ. However, because of God's goodness and mercy, these babies live forever in a state of heaven-like bliss in limbo. They do not burn in hell.

Modern: I agree with the Puritanical and Calvinistic teachings of those modern Christian churches that teach that such unworthy and unclean babies live forever in hell. Actually, all men and women are born inherently evil and thus are worthy only of hell. It is only by the grace of God that a few are selected from among the "mass of perdition" to be saved with Him in heaven.

Ancient and Restored: I agree with the teachings of original Christianity that children come into this world spotless and clean. As they grow older and become accountable for their actions before God, through accepting and living the principles and ordinances of the gospel of Jesus Christ they can prove themselves worthy to return to God. As an infant or little child, they are innocent and pure before God and have no need for baptism. Unless we ourselves become pure like little children, we will not enter into the kingdom of heaven.

Note: Many early church leaders attacked Augustine's new theory of original sin, not believing that a just, loving, and merciful God would hold a baby accountable for a sin committed by someone else and of which they obviously could not repent. However, to defend this new theory and doctrine, Augustine would continually quote from Romans 5:12, which in the Latin Vulgate version of the Bible that he used reads, "Propterea sicut per unum hominem peccatum in hunc mundum intravit, et per peccatum mors, pertransiit, in quo onmes peccaverunt" (Wherefore, as by one man sin entered into the world, and death by sin; and so death passed upon all men, in whom all have sinned).[22]

NOTES

1. *Jefferson's Complete Works*, vol. 7, 210, 257, quoted in *The Falling Away and Restoration of the Gospel of Jesus Christ Foretold* (Salt Lake City: The Church of Jesus Christ of Latter-day Saints, 1976).

2. John Lawrence Mosheim, *An Ecclesiastical History, Ancient and Modern*, vol. 1, James Murdock, trans. (London: William Tegg and Co., 1859), 153–54.

3. John Henry Newman, "An Essay on the Development of Christian Doctrine," 1878, 269–70, quoted in Alvin R. Dyer, *The Challenge* (Sat Lake City: Deseret Book, 1962), 195–96; italics added.

4. *Cambridge Bible Dictionary*, 135–36.

5. John Henry Newman, "An Essay on the Development of Christian Doctrine," 1878, 269–70, quoted in Dyer, *The Challenge*, 195–96.

6. Edward Gibbon, *The Decline and Fall of the Roman Empire* (New York, Heritage Press, 1946), 169–72.

7. Robertson, *History of the Christian Church*, ii, 50, quoted in Clark, *On the Way to Immortality and Eternal Life* (Salt Lake City: Deseret Book, 1953), 297.

8. Schaff, *History of the Christian Church*, iv, 451, quoted in Clark, *On the Way*, 295.

9. Franz Funk, *A Manual of Church History*, vol. 1, 297–98, quoted in Barker, *Apostasy*, 694.

10. Clark, *On the Way*, 284.

11. Ibid., 284–85.

12. Gibbon, *The Decline and Fall of the Roman Empire*, 311–13.

13. Clark, *On the Way*, 286–87.

14. James H. Robinson, *An Introduction to the History of Western Europe*, vol. 1, 390, quoted in Barker, *Apostasy*, 694.

15. Schaff, *History of the Christian Church*, vol. 7, 607–9, quoted in Clark, *On the Way*, 288–91.

16. Philip Schaff, *History of the Christian Church*, vol. 8 (Grand Rapids, MI: Wm. B. Eerdmans Publishing, 1958), 252.

17. Martin Luther, quoted in James E. Talmage, *The Great Apostasy* (Salt Lake City: Deseret Book, 1968), 127.

18. Bruce R. McConkie, *A New Witness for the Articles of Faith* (Salt Lake City: Deseret Book, 1976), 101.

19. Louis Duchesne, *Histoire Ancienne de l'Eglise*, vol. 3, 204, quoted in Barker, *Apostasy*, 181–82.

20. Crampon, *La Sainte Bible*, 178, note, quoted in Barker, *Apostasy*, 441.

21. Schaff, *History of the Christian Church*, vol. 3, 834, quoted in Barker, *Apostasy*, 441.

22. Barker, *Apostasy*, 440.

Section III
The True Nature
of God

QUESTION #6

According to the widely accepted doctrine of the Holy Trinity, Jesus Christ is God the Father who, taking upon Himself human form and a physical body, became the Son of God. If Jesus and His Father are actually one and the same Being, why did Christ spend many hours, and even forty days in the wilderness, praying to Himself for divine direction?

ORIGINAL CHRISTIAN TEACHINGS

In the early years of Christianity, it was commonly understood and taught that the Father and the Son were two totally separate and distinct divine Beings. The New Testament record contains a number of examples that confirm this truth: Jesus spent many hours in fervent prayer, communing with His Father; the voice of the Father was heard from the heavens at the time of Jesus' baptism, witnessing to those present that Jesus was indeed His beloved Son (see Matthew 3:16–17); and the disciple Stephen saw both the Father and the Son in a vision just prior to his death by stoning: "But he [Stephen], being full of the Holy Ghost, looked up stedfastly into heaven, and saw the glory of God, and *Jesus standing on the right hand of God*, And said, Behold, I see the heavens opened, and the Son of man standing on the right hand of God" (Acts 7:55–56; italics added).

Here Stephen saw *two* distinct divine Beings, the Savior standing on the "right hand" (meaning the right side) of His Father.

Although Jesus Himself is a divine Being—one of the three members of the Godhead—He openly admitted, "My Father is greater than

I" (John 14:28). He came to earth to do the will of His Father, and at the time of His resurrection let Mary and the apostles know that their God was the same as His: "Jesus saith unto her, Touch me not; for I am not yet ascended to my Father: but go to my brethren, and say unto them, I ascend unto my Father, and your Father; and to my God, and your God" (John 20:17).

Some are confused, however, by Christ's statement "I and my Father are one" (John 10:30). Was Jesus here declaring that He and His Father were one and the same Being, as modern Christianity teaches us today? The Savior clarified His teachings on this matter, of course, while praying to His Father in behalf of His apostles: "And now I am no more in the world, but these are in the world, and I come to thee. Holy Father, keep through thine own name those whom thou hast given me, that *they may be one, as we are*. . . . Neither pray I for these alone, but for them also which will believe on me through their word; That they may *all be one*; as thou, Father, art in me, and I in thee, *that they also may be one in us*; that the world may believe that thou hast sent me" (John 17:11, 20–22; italics added).

Obviously, it was not the Savior's intent that His disciples become physically joined into one being, but rather that they be united in purpose, thought, and action—in the very same manner that the Savior and His Father, while existing physically as two separate and distinct Beings, are nevertheless perfectly united and in harmony with one another in purpose, thought, and action.

Early Christian leaders who wrote concerning the nature of Deity similarly understood these simple truths. For example, this distinction of persons was taught by such church leaders as Novatian (about AD 251), Hippolytus (AD 165–236), Saint Justin (Justin Martyr, AD 100–166), and many others.

> The Verb, [Word] who later will be Jesus Christ, is the Son of God. . . . Hence and by virtue of this generation, the Son is distinct from the Father. This distinction is placed more or less in relief by the Apologists: Saint Justin strongly insists on it. In relation to God the Creator, the Son is another, another as to number, although in accord with him. He is not distinguished from him by name only, as the light is distinguished from the sun, but he is numerically something else. . . . Tatian and Athenagoras use equivalent expressions.[1]

> Justin Martyr says that the Son is *eteron ti*, something other, from

the Father; and Tertullian affirms, *Filium et Patrem esse aliud ab alio*, with the same intent as Hippolytus here, viz.: to express the distinction of persons.[2]

MEDIEVAL AND MODERN CHRISTIAN TEACHINGS

Today, of course, a much different concept of God is taught by modern Christian churches. The teachings of early Christian leaders on this subject are greatly criticized by theologians in our day. For example, the supposed errors of these early churchmen are soundly denounced by the Roman Catholic historian Hefele:

> The Apologists [early Christian writers who wrote in defense of the Church's teachings during the second century and first half of the third] placed too low an estimate on the Son in regard to His divinity and power; they attributed to His Being a beginning, and consequently did not recognize His equality with the Father (thus, Athanagorus and Theophilus; Tatian, Tertullian, and especially Origen), and *emphasized too much the personal distinction from the Father.*[3]

As Hefele and other modern Christian scholars and historians readily admit, virtually all early Christian writers greatly stressed the fact that the Son was literally begotten by the Father and that the two were totally separate divine Beings.

During the first centuries of the Christian era, contemporary worldly philosophers and their students had greatly ridiculed Christianity as merely another form of polytheism—the worship of many gods. In spite of the criticism, early Christian leaders would continually and emphatically declare the members of the Godhead to be totally separate from one another. As the centuries passed, however, many new converts, highly trained in worldly philosophy, would join the Church. By early in the fourth century, rather than continue to fight the false philosophies of the world, over three hundred bishops gathered at the Council of Nicea (AD 325) seeking to create a God that would silence the critics and satisfy the teachings of *both* the Christian and the pagan systems of belief.

Early Christian leaders had taught that the Father and the Son were two totally separate and distinct divine Beings. The ancient Greek philosopher Plato (400 BC), however, had taught that there was only one divine Being. As a compromise, at Nicea, Christian bishops determined that the Christian belief concerning the nature of God and the pagan Greek philosophical belief concerning the nature of God, even though contradictory to each other, were nonetheless both true. How it was that two totally separate Beings could at the same time be one Being could never be reasonably explained, of course. Thus, the doctrine of the Trinity, which affirms one contradiction after another, would be declared at Nicea, even as it is today, an incomprehensible mystery.

The Athanasian Creed, which was developed during this period, is typical of this very confusing description of deity held even today by virtually all modern Christian sects. Note carefully how the authors of the Creed first state a Christian belief concerning the nature of the Godhead, but then quickly qualify this statement with an offsetting statement affirming Plato's pagan, philosophical view of deity. We see these contradictions being repeated over and over again. The Creed reads as follows,

> We worship one God in Trinity, and Trinity in Unity, neither confounding the persons, nor dividing the substance. For there is one person of the Father, another of the Son, and another of the Holy Ghost. But the Godhead of the Father, Son, and Holy Ghost, is all one: the glory equal, the majesty coeternal. Such as the Father is, such is the Son, and such is the Holy Ghost. The Father uncreate, the Son uncreate, and the Holy Ghost uncreate. The Father incomprehensible, the Son incomprehensible, and the Holy Ghost incomprehensible. The Father eternal, the Son eternal, and the Holy Ghost eternal. And yet there are not three eternals, but one eternal. As also there are not three incomprehensibles, nor three uncreated; but one uncreated, and one incomprehensible. So likewise the Father is Almighty, the Son Almighty, and the Holy Ghost Almighty; and yet there are not three Almighties, but one Almighty. So the Father is God, the Son is God, and the Holy Ghost is God, and yet there are not three Gods but one God.[4]

Commenting upon this Creed, James E. Talmage notes, "It would be difficult to conceive of a greater number of inconsistencies and contradictions, expressed in words as few."[5]

As we would expect, the final result of this courtship and ultimate marriage of Christian doctrine and pagan philosophy was indeed a muddled mysticism.

> In the early centuries of the Christian era, the apostasy came not through persecution, but by relinquishment of faith caused by the superimposing of a man-made structure upon and over the divine program. Many men with no pretense nor claim to revelation, speaking without divine authority or revelation, depending only upon their own

brilliant minds, but representing as they claim the congregations of the Christians and in long conference and erudite [scholarly] councils, sought the creation process to make a God which all could accept.

The brilliant minds with their philosophies, knowing much about Christian traditions and . . . pagan philosophies, would combine all elements to please everybody. They replaced the simple ways and program of Christ with spectacular rituals, colorful display, impressive pageantry, and limitless pomposity, and called it Christianity. They had replaced the glorious, divine plan of exaltation of Christ with an elaborate, colorful, man-made system. They seemed to have little idea of totally dethroning Christ, nor terminating the life of God, as in our own day, but they put together an incomprehensible God idea.

They thus reached the point of muddled mysticism called "the mystery of mysteries," with contradictions that Gods are separate yet combined, substance yet without substance, anthropomorphic [possessing human form] yet only spirit, the Son begotten yet unbegottten.

It took them years to develop this incomprehensible mysticism, and after many centuries the Christians are still mystified, and this has led in no small measure to the "Death of God" theorists, for as one modern thinker said: "It is easier to think of a dead God than one who is mystified, disembodied, inactivated, powerless, unimpressive."[6]

CHRIST'S ORIGINAL TEACHINGS RESTORED TO JOSEPH SMITH

Even as a young, fourteen-year-old boy, Joseph Smith was well aware of the concept of God being taught by the Christian churches of his day. Had he been attempting to deceive others in his community, he might have declared that he had seen a bright formless light—or perhaps had simply seen and spoken to the Savior. Even if such claims had been untrue, at least his description would have been consistent with the universally accepted beliefs of his day concerning deity. But instead, Joseph declared that he had seen *two* distinct Beings and described them both as being in human form.

Such a description of the Godhead was totally unheard of in his day. And yet, with such a description, how simple and clear the teachings of the holy scriptures suddenly appear! For example, now we realize that man truly was made "in the image and likeness of God"—in other words, we really do look like Him, just as the scriptures declare. (See Genesis 1:26–27.) The Savior actually is "the express image" of His Father—He really does look just like His Father. (See Hebrews 1:3.) It really was possible for the prophet Moses to speak "face to face" with God, even "as a man speaketh unto his friend" (Exodus 33:11). The disciple Stephen really did see two divine Beings—"the Son of man standing on the right hand of God" (Acts 7:56). God really was assisted by at least one other Being in the creation process, declaring, "Let us make man in our image" (Genesis 1:26; see also 3:22). Christ really did spend many hours praying to His Father—not to Himself!

Joseph would also learn that although there had been many ancient prophets—such as Isaiah (see Isaiah 6:1, 5), Moses (see Exodus 24:10), and Jacob (see Genesis 32:30)—who had seen God "face to face" (Exodus 33:11), the average man is sent to earth to prove his obedience to God, living by faith, not by sight. Thus, for mankind in general, "God is a spirit" (John 4:24), meaning that we do not talk to Him "face to face" as do the prophets. Rather, we come to know Him through His Spirit, or divine influence and intelligence, that radiates from Him, enlightening our minds with truth.

Thus we see that, unlike the mysterious and unreasonable teachings of modern Christianity, the teachings of original, pure Christianity as revealed anew to mankind through the Prophet Joseph Smith are so very easy to understand—and they actually make sense.

QUESTION #7

The Bible teaches that "no man hath seen God at any time" (John 1:18). If this is true, how can Joseph Smith, or any other person, claim to have ever seen Him?

The Bible makes it very clear that it *is* possible for men to see God and provides us with many examples where this did actually take place. It thus seems quite confusing when the apostle John appears to contradict these Biblical teachings by stating, "No man hath seen God at any time; the only begotten Son, which is in the bosom of the Father, he hath declared him" (John 1:18; see also 1 John 4:12).

The Prophet Joseph Smith learned that although John's statement has not come down to us exactly as it was originally written (apparently it was corrupted in medieval times to provide support for Christianity's new Platonic concept of God), even as the verse now stands it still teaches us a great truth if properly understood. For just as John knew, Joseph learned that no man in his normal, mortal condition has ever seen God nor indeed can see Him—for such a man would be consumed by God's very presence. These truths were revealed anew to the prophet Joseph by the Savior and clarified in this manner: "For no man has seen God at any time in the flesh, except quickened by the Spirit of God" (D&C 67:11).

The physical senses of our current mortal bodies possess certain limitations. For example, a dog whistle emits sound waves at frequencies that are clearly discernible to a dog but cannot be heard by a human. A hawk gliding hundreds of feet in the air can clearly see a rabbit or even a small mouse moving about far below, whereas at this same distance you and I would be unable to see either one. Certain objects are too far away for us to see without the aid of a telescope, and other objects are too small for us to see without the aid of a microscope. Our mortal eyes cannot see God without the aid of the Holy Ghost.

A mortal person, in their normal mortal condition, cannot see God, for as the apostle Paul taught us, He is an "invisible God" (Colossians 1:14–15). However, the scriptures further make clear that when a man or woman is overshadowed by the influence of the Holy Ghost, it is most definitely possible to see God. "But he [Stephen] *being full of the Holy Ghost* . . . saw the glory of God, and Jesus standing on the right hand of God" (Acts 7:55–56). Obviously, had those who were in the process of stoning Stephen been able to see what he witnessed, they would have quickly dropped their stones. But while Stephen, "being full of the Holy Ghost," could plainly see the glorified, resurrected Christ and His Father, to those others who were present, both the Father and the Son were invisible.

The Old Testament prophet Daniel had a similar experience when he saw God in vision and then stated, "And I Daniel alone saw the vision: for the men that were with me saw not the vision; but a great quaking fell upon them, so that they fled to hide themselves" (Daniel 10:7). Apparently, to those who were present with Daniel when this glorious manifestation took place, God was invisible.

In a somewhat similar fashion, Saul (who later became the apostle Paul), while on his way to the city of Damascus, beheld and spoke to the resurrected Lord when the Savior appeared to him within a great and glorious light. The scriptural account of this event, however, indicates that the men who were journeying with Saul did not see what he beheld: "And the men which journeyed with him stood speechless, hearing a voice, but seeing no man" (Acts 9:7).

Thus, while Saul (Paul) actually saw the risen Christ in all of His glory, to the others who were present, the Savior was invisible. It was this knowledge that undoubtedly caused Paul to speak of God as an "invisible God," while fully understanding that righteous men, when under the influence of the Holy Ghost, could indeed see God. Thus Paul spoke of the prophet Moses as having actually seen the invisible God: "By faith he [Moses] forsook Egypt, not fearing the wrath of the king: for he endured, as *seeing him who is invisible*" (Hebrews 11:27; italics added).

Of course, only a privileged few are allowed such a blessing as to actually behold God. As we earlier noted, mankind in general is not permitted to stand in His presence, for they would be consumed by His glory. "For there will no man see me, and live" (Exodus 33:20), God had declared to a disobedient Israelite nation. But, nevertheless, His appointed servant Moses, being overshadowed by the Holy Ghost, was allowed and able to both see and speak directly to the very God of Israel. "And the Lord spake unto Moses face to face, as a man speaketh unto his friend" (Exodus 33:11).

While the average mortal man could not have survived such an encounter, Moses was transfigured before the Lord and his life was preserved. When he came down from Mount Sinai after seeing God, the scriptures state that "his face shone" (Exodus 34:29), a portion of God's glory still resting upon him.

Although the apostle John understood and declared that no unrighteous man—or even a righteous man in his normal mortal condition—had ever seen God, he also knew that righteous men, under the influence of the Holy Ghost can and do see God: "It is written in the prophets, And they will be all taught of God. Every man therefore that hath heard, and hath learned of the Father cometh unto me. Not that any man hath seen the Father, *save he which is of God, he hath seen the Father*" (John 6:45–46; italics added).

Thus, the Savior indicated that for those individuals who are "of God," it truly is possible to see the Father. John himself, of course, was obviously one of these righteous men whom the Savior described as being "of God," for the scriptures record that John had been permitted to see both the Father and the Son in vision, Christ standing before His Father as God sat upon His throne in heaven. (See Revelation 4 and 5.) Of course, during this marvelous revelation, John describes himself as having been "in the Spirit" (Revelation 1:10), that is, under the influence of the Holy Ghost.

God the Father and God the Son have both been seen during ancient and modern times but, as we will next discuss, it is God the Son (Jesus Christ) who has been seen most frequently.

QUESTION #8

In the Old Testament, the God of ancient Israel was named Jehovah. Who exactly is He? Is He our Heavenly Father? Is He the Holy Trinity—that is, the Father, Son, and Holy Ghost all rolled into one divine Being? Or is He someone else?

ORIGINAL CHRISTIAN TEACHINGS

In the early Christian Church, it was clearly understood and taught that Jesus Christ stood as the mediator between God and mankind. He alone, as the Savior of the world, held this unique position. The truth of this fact was noted by the apostle Paul as follows: "There is one God, and one mediator between God and men, the man Jesus Christ" (1 Timothy 2:5).

In his role as mediator, the Savior acts as an advocate before the Father, pleading the cause of the righteous in the courts of heaven. As taught by the apostle John, "My little children, these things I write unto you, that ye sin not. And if any man sin, we have an advocate with the Father, Jesus Christ the righteous" (1 John 2:1).

Indeed, not only was Christ chosen to serve as the one mediator and advocate for mankind, He was also assigned by the Father to act as the eternal judge of all God's children: "For the Father judgeth no man, but hath committed all judgment unto the Son" (John 5:22).

Being placed between God and man as the mediator, advocate, judge, and savior of mankind, Jesus Christ was assigned by God to work *directly* with the Father's children, revealing God's will and plan of salvation to them. In this unique role, it was Jesus Christ (known in ancient times as Jehovah) who personally appeared to the prophets of old, as recorded in the Old Testament record. This truth was commonly understood and taught by early Christian leaders and writers. For example, concerning Jehovah, the God of the Old Testament who delivered Israel from the bondage of the Egyptians and followed the camp of Israel in the desert, the apostle Paul would declare, "Moreover, brethren, I would not that ye should be ignorant, how that all our fathers were under the cloud, and all passed through the [Red] sea; And were all baptized unto Moses in the cloud and in the sea; And did all eat the same spiritual meat; And did all drink the same spiritual drink: for they drank of that *spiritual Rock that followed them: and that Rock was Christ*" (1 Corinthians 10:1–4; italics added).

The early Christian writers of the first three centuries AD similarly understood this truth. For example, "But Jesus is indeed he who appeared and spoke to Moses, to Abraham and in a word, to all the other patriarchs, to serve the will of his Father; it is he who came to be born a man by the Virgin Mary, and he is one still."[7]

Similarly, we have the teachings of Irenaeus, bishop of Lyons (a city in what is now modern-day France), a prominent church leader in his day who had been taught by Polycarp, who in turn, had been taught directly by the apostle John. As Irenaeus notes,

> For not alone upon Abraham's account did he say these things, but also that he might point out how all who have known God from the beginning, and have foretold the advent of Christ, have received the revelation from the Son himself. . . .
>
> Therefore have the Jews departed from God, in not receiving his word, but imagining that they could know the Father (apart) by himself, without the Word, that is, without the Son; they being ignorant of that God who spake in human shape to Abraham, and again to Moses, saying, "I have surely seen the affliction of my people in Egypt, and I have come down to deliver them." For the Son, who is the word of God, arranged these things aforehand from the beginning.[8]

THE TEACHINGS OF CHRISTIANITY IN THE MIDDLE AND MODERN AGES

Commenting upon the teachings of early Christian church leaders on this subject, the Roman Catholic historian Fernand Mourett notes the following: "Nothing is remarkable like the insistence with which Saint Justin, (died a martyr in Rome 166), Theophilus of Antioch (died 190), Saint Irenaeus (about 200), Tertullian (160–220), Clement of Alexandria (150–211), and Origen (185–243), repeat insistently that it is the Verb (Jesus) who revealed himself to men in the divine appearance of the Old Testament."[9]

The teachings of these early church leaders seem so remarkable to Mourett and so many other modern religious scholars because so many modern Christian churches no longer teach these simple, basic truths, having lost an understanding of the true nature of—and relationship between—Christ and His Father, since early in the fourth century. Not only did men lose an understanding of Christ's premortal relationship with His Father, but they totally lost sight of His unique role as the sole mediator and advocate between the Father and mankind.

The teachings of the Christian church, in the Middle Ages, with emphasis on original sin, the corrupt nature of man and the anger of God toward the sinner, tended to widen the breech between man and God. Mortals came to fear that God would not hear a prayer from their sinful lips and they sought help from intermediaries. It became common for sinners to address a prayer to a saint, asking the saint to pray for them. Gradually this practice, with church encouragement and regulation, assumed an organized aspect. The saints were spoken of as "advocates" of the sinner before the throne of God. This is the Latin word for lawyer or attorney and the saint assumed the role of a lawyer pleading the case of the sinner before God who was demanding vengeance for sin.

There is another school of thought which finds an explanation of this practice as a survival of paganism. In antiquity, the people had sought the aid of local gods who were also often specialists in some particular thing, to gain favor of Zeus on their behalf. A counterpart is found in the Christian practice of seeking this intercession. God (or Christ) took the place of Zeus in Christianity, and the saints succeeded the lesser gods. For example, St. Nicholas became the specialist in protecting children, making them happy, aiding students and helping girls without dowries acquire husbands; St. Christopher was the special protector of travelers; St. Lucy was sought after by those with failing vision and St. Luke was the favorite of the doctors.[10]

As previously noted, the scriptures very plainly teach that there is only "one mediator between God and men, the man Jesus Christ" (1 Timothy 2:5). Also, "we have an advocate with the Father, Jesus Christ the righteous" (1 John 2:1). As the true nature of the Father and the Son, existing as two totally separate divine Beings, was replaced by Plato's theory that there was only one divine Being, Christ ceased to be the "one mediator" between the Father and mankind. Instead, Christ suddenly became the Father Himself. The saints then took the place of Christ, serving as mediators between God/Christ and men. This, of course, was a total perversion of original Christian teachings.

During the Middle Ages there seemed to be scarcely a single Christian doctrine that could remain pure and untainted from pagan practice or belief, or that was anything more than simply a man-made invention. As the centuries passed and pagan philosophies continued to replace the pure teachings of Christ, Christianity slipped ever further into spiritual darkness.

CHRIST'S ORIGINAL TEACHINGS RESTORED TO JOSEPH SMITH

If the Lord's true church were on the earth today, I would expect it to teach that there is only one mediator between God and man—even our Lord and Savior, Jesus Christ. The leaders of this church would teach, even as did all Christian church leaders anciently, that prior to His birth into mortality, Jesus Christ was He who appeared to the prophets of old, being called in ancient times Jehovah.

In this true church, there would be no worship of or praying to mediators or dead saints. There would be no attempt to embrace or copy pagan practices of worship in order to appease the pagan appetites of the people.

It is interesting to note that during the appearance of the Father and the Son to the Prophet Joseph Smith, known as the First Vision, that the Father introduced and bore witness that Jesus was indeed His "Beloved Son," but that it was the Son—not the Father—who instructed the young prophet. Why not the Father? Because it is the Son who is the mediator and has been assigned the responsibility of instructing the Father's children and of leading them back to His presence. At a later time, Joseph would learn that the Son truly was the Jehovah of the Old Testament record, the mediator between God and man, having revealed Himself as the Savior of mankind long before entering mortal life. "I, even I, am the Lord; and beside me there is no saviour" (Isaiah 43:11), Jehovah had declared. (See also Isaiah 45:21; Hosea 13:4.) Similarly, it was Christ who had declared Himself unto Moses to be the great "I AM" (Exodus 3:14).

With this restored understanding of Christ's premortal role as Jehovah, many Biblical passages become much clearer to us. For example, on one occasion during His mortal ministry, the Savior was found preaching in the temple to some unbelieving Jews who were boasting of their special heritage as descendents of the prophet Abraham. In response to such claims Jesus declared, "Verily, verily, I say unto you, Before Abraham was, I AM" (John 8:58). After stating this, the Biblical account records that the Jews "took . . . up stones to cast at him" (John 8:59).

The Savior's statement seems a bit confusing, but certainly not cause for being stoned to death. However, today we know that the meaning of this scriptural passage had become corrupted and largely lost during the Middle Ages. The message the Savior had actually conveyed to His listeners was, "Verily, verily, I say unto you, Before Abraham, was I AM."[11] In other words, Jesus had declared Himself to be "I AM"—the God of the

Old Testament. Such a claim was so blasphemous as it fell upon the ears of these unbelieving Jews, we can now see why they immediately took up stones, seeking to kill Him!

How blessed we are today to have restored to earth a true understanding of God, and of Jesus' true relationship with His—and our—Father.

QUESTION #9

You say that modern Christianity's concept of deity has largely been taken from the teachings of the ancient Greek philosopher Plato. What exactly did Plato teach concerning the nature of God?

Throughout the Holy Bible, we are taught that God is a personal Being. It was God the Father who walked and talked with Adam and Eve in the Garden of Eden. (See Genesis 3:8.) Once they had transgressed His commandment and partaken of the forbidden fruit, however, they were no longer worthy to stand in His presence. The job of redeeming fallen man, and of helping individuals to become worthy to reenter God's presence, then fell upon the shoulders of the mediator or Savior. Thus, it was God the Son, or Jehovah, who spoke "face to face" with the prophet Moses (see Exodus 33:11), who was seen by seventy elders of Israel on Mount Sinai (see Exodus 24:9–11), and who was described as being in the form of a man by the prophet Ezekiel (see Ezekiel 1:26–28), as well as by a host of other prophets to whom He personally appeared. These Biblical teachings and similar teachings of the early Christian leaders were greatly criticized and even ridiculed by the contemporary philosophers and intellectuals of their day. For example, Celsus, a very bitter anti-Christian writer of the second century, declared,

> The Christians say that God has hands, a mouth, and a voice; they are always proclaiming that "God said this" or "God spoke." "The heavens declare the work of his hands," they say. I can only comment that such a God is no god at all, for God has neither hands, mouth, nor voice, nor any characteristics of which we know. And they say that God made man in his own image, failing to realize that God is not at all like a man, nor vice versa; God resembles no form known to us. They say that God has form, namely the form of the Logos, who became flesh in Jesus Christ. But we know that God is without shape, without color. They say that God moved above the waters he created—but we know that it is contrary to the nature of God to move. Their absurd doctrines even contain reference to God walking about in the garden he created

for man; and they speak of him being angry, jealous, moved to repentance, sorry, sleepy—in short, as being in every aspect more a man than
a God. They have not read Plato, who teaches us in the *Republic* that
God (the Good) does not even participate in being.[12]

In commenting upon Celsus's criticism of early Christian teachings,
religious scholar Joseph F. McConkie muses, "So now we get to the heart
of the matter. The problem with these poor ignorant Christians is that
they have been reading the words of the prophets instead of the teachings
of Plato."[13]

Unfortunately, in the ensuing years, Christian church leaders *did* read
Plato, with the result that today modern Christian scholars and leaders
have taken the place of Celsus and other anti-Christian writers of his day
in criticizing the teachings of these early Christian leaders. Thus we see an
entirely different gospel being taught today, the gospel according to Plato
replacing the gospel according to God's apostles and prophets.

Unlike the understanding of the nature of God possessed by early
Christians, which had come through divine revelation by God to His
appointed apostles and prophets, Plato and the other ancient Greek philosophers did not believe in divine revelation or that God could, or ever
would, actually speak to man. Rather, Plato believed that everything
about God and His nature could be discovered by means of the great
reasoning power that God had placed within man himself.

To more fully understand how Plato (using human reason and not
divine revelation) developed his new concept of deity, which would eventually be adopted by medieval Christianity, one must have some understanding of his concept of reality. The following explanation may seem
quite confusing or incomprehensible, but this in itself may help us begin
to understand why the doctrine of the Holy Trinity, as later formulated
by the reasoning of Christian theologians, is equally so confusing and
incomprehensible to us today.

> For Plato, an object consists of the "form" or "idea" and the matter
> or material of which it is made. The ideas of beauty, justice, good-
> ness, etc., which for us are abstractions, are for Plato realities. In other
> words, for us, the good, the beautiful, the just, are abstract ideas, which
> do not exist apart from the object. But for Plato these abstract ideas are
> the realities. The objects with which they are associated are perishable,
> therefore the greater reality for him, is the "idea" or "form" back of the
> object.

For Plato, the Supreme Being is absolute goodness, and since matter, for him, is evil and a hindrance to the perfect expression of the idea, "God is immaterial."[14]

The God of Plato is neither inferior nor superior to the idea . . . he coincides with it . . . he is the Idea itself, considered as an active, plastic, and creative principle. . . .

Does this mean that because his god is an Idea he is not reality? On the contrary, because he is an Idea, and nothing but an Idea, he is the highest reality; for, from Plato's point of view, the Idea only is real.[15]

Thus, for example, we may look at a flower and say that it is beautiful. But, for Plato, the actual physical, material flower that we can see, touch, and smell is not real. Once the physical flower dies and withers away, however, beauty still remains—it is real. The idea of beauty is, in essence, alive even though one cannot see, touch, or smell it. For Plato, it is such abstract concepts as beauty, justice, and goodness that truly do exist and are real.

Not wishing to be disrespectful towards this ancient Greek thinker, but in all seriousness, if such teachings had first originated with some-one living in our own modern day and age, they very likely would have been scorned to shame and their mental state seriously questioned. What comes to mind is the vision of a man holding a long butterfly net, chasing and swinging his net at some formless, elusive, invisible mist.

Since physical matter (for some unknown reason) was considered evil by Plato, God (what he called the Good) obviously could not be asso-ciated with any form of matter. Thus, God could only be an idea, or in other words, an immaterial, ethereal nothingness living on a plane of existence totally outside of our own. Furthermore, possessing no physical shape or body, it was impossible for God to be seen or to have any physical sensations, impressions, emotions, or feelings. Indeed, Plato's was a god without body, parts, or passions.

John Adams and Thomas Jefferson, the second and third presidents of the United States, were political adversaries during much of their adult lives. In their later years, however, they became the best of friends. They would regularly write one another, discussing matters of science, philosophy, government, and religion. After having read the teachings of Plato, from which medieval Christianity formed its new concept of deity, Jefferson wrote the following to his dear friend Adams:

> His [Plato's] foggy mind, is forever presenting the semblances of objects which, half seen thro' a mist, can be defined neither in form or dimension. Yet this which should have consigned him to early oblivion really procured him immortality of fame and reverence. The Christian priesthood, finding the doctrines of Christ leveled to every understanding, and too plain to need explanation, saw, in the mysticisms of Plato, materials with which they might build up an artificial system which might, from its indistinctness, admit everlasting controversy, give employment for their order, and introduce it to profit, power and pre-eminence. The doctrines which flowed from the lips of Jesus himself are within the comprehension of a child; but thousands of volumes have not yet explained the Platonisms engrafted on them: and for this obvious reason that nonsense can never be explained. Their purposes however are answered. Plato is canonized; and it is now deemed as impious to question his merits as those of an apostle of Jesus. He is peculiarly appealed to as an advocate of the immortality of the soul; and yet I will venture to say that were there no better arguments than his in proof of it, not a man in the world would believe it. It is fortunate for us that Platonic republicanism has not obtained the same favor as Platonic Christianity; or we should now have been . . . living, men, women and children, pell mell together, like beasts of the field or forest.[16]

As Christian theologians came to accept the teachings of Plato, it required that the Bible be interpreted in an entirely new way. For example, the scriptures teach us that "God is love" (1 John 4:8), a divine Being who cares for His children, who is merciful and compassionate. He feels sorrow, disappointment, or even righteous indignation when His children sin, and He feels happiness and joy when they are obedient to His commandments. Yet we are not to be confused and think that He is able to actually *feel* any of these emotions like we do—for the immaterial God of Plato and modern Christendom has no emotions, feelings, or passions as we know them.

Furthermore, we have been commanded by Christ to be "perfect, even as [our] Father which is in heaven is perfect" (Matthew 5:48). Similarly, the apostle John tells us that if we live righteously we will one day see God and realize that we are indeed like him. (See 1 John 3:2.) Today, however, modern Christian scholars tell us not to take these teachings too literally; for in the first place, according to Plato, God cannot be seen (apparently the ancient prophets were just kidding around when they wrote that they had actually seen and spoken to Him); and in the second place, we can no more become like him than a worm can become like a horse. Indeed, it appears that once one has accepted the God of the Greek philosophers, nothing in the scriptures can be trusted to actually mean what it says. Just about everything must be understood figuratively or as a metaphor. Indeed, anything in holy writ that speaks of God, and of our relationship to Him, suddenly becomes an incomprehensible mystery.

In order to reconcile Plato's beliefs with Christianity, both medieval and modern Christian theologians have been required to employ "the grand key of mischief." As Joseph F. McConkie explains,

> Theologically the issue divides itself into two parts—*anthropomorphism*, that is, ascribing human form to God, and *anthropopathism*, that is, ascribing human feelings, attitudes, or passions to God. The God of the scriptures is both anthropomorphic and anthropopathic, while the God of traditional [modern] Christianity is neither. Thus the question becomes, Do you adjust your belief to the scriptures or the scriptures to your belief? [Modern Christian churches] . . . have chosen to adjust the scriptures to their [Platonic] belief. This is where the grand key of mischief proves so helpful. All that they need do to accomplish this is to designate the literal as figurative and where necessary the figurative as literal.[17]

In speaking of the determined effort of early Christian leaders to reconcile their beliefs with popular worldly philosophy and thus gain the stamp of approval from pagan intellectuals, McConkie further notes,

> What was most keenly desired on the part of Christians of that era [early fourth century AD] was respectability in the Graeco-Roman world. It was not peaceful cohabitation with the world that they sought but reconciliation. They sought to defend the faith on philosophical grounds so they could prove it worthy of the attention of pagan intellectuals. Thus philosophy became the disinfectant used to rid Christianity of the anthropomorphic notion that God resembled man and to disallow a literal reading of the many passages of scripture that describe personal encounters with Him. The testimony of God's covenant spokesmen [the writings of the prophets] was determined to be metaphor or allegory and thus subject to any distortion imposed upon it.
>
> Thus reason supplanted revelation, scholars replaced prophets, a formless and incomprehensible God deposed the God who created Adam and Eve in his image and likeness, and loyalty to creeds became

the measure of faith in preference to holiness. The Bible became an allegory, its most sacred truths became a mystery, and mankind ceased to be heirs of God, becoming instead mere toys created for the amusement of heaven.[18]

Were it not for the personal appearance of the Father and the Son to the Prophet Joseph Smith, restoring once again to earth a correct understanding of the true nature of the members of the Godhead, and the true relationship our Heavenly Father has with His children, mankind would have forever remained in the spiritual Dark Ages of time.

Now, What Do You Believe?

If Jesus and His Father are, in essence, one and the same Being, why did He spend so much time praying to Himself for divine direction? (Mentally, check one of these two answers.)

Modern: I agree with the teachings of medieval and modern Christianity that, combining both Christian doctrine and Plato's philosophical theories, declare Christ and the Father to be separate and yet combined; totally different and yet one and the same Being. And, thus, they are totally incomprehensible. Why did Christ spend many hours and even forty days fasting and praying to Himself for divine direction? We do not know, of course, for the human mind cannot comprehend God, nor even begin to understand His mysterious ways.

Ancient and Restored: I agree with the teachings of the Bible and virtually all of the early Christian Church leaders, that Christ and His Father are not the same, but rather two totally separate and distinct divine Beings. Christ was begotten of the Father, is in His image, and in thought and purpose is in perfect accord with Him. He came to earth to do the will of the Father. Through prayer and divine revelation, He received encouragement and guidance from the Father, thus enabling Him to fully accomplish His divine mission on earth.

Notes

1. Tixeront, *Histoire des Dogmas*, vol. 1, 247, quoted in Barker, *Apostasy*, 43.
2. Hippolytus, *Against the Heresy of Noetus*, translator's note, quoted in Barker, *Apostasy*, 44.
3. Hefele, *Histoire des Conciles*, vol. 1, pt. 1, 337–38, quoted in Barker, *Apostasy*, 266; italics added.
4. Athanasian Creed, quoted in James E. Talmage, *The Great Apostasy* (Salt Lake City: Deseret Book, 1968), 104.

5. James E. Talmage, *Articles of Faith* (Salt Lake City: Deseret Book, 1984), 48.

6. Spencer W. Kimball, *The Teachings of Spencer W. Kimball*, (Salt Lake City: Bookcraft, 1982), 425–26.

7. Justin Martyr, *Dialogue with Trypho*, cxiii, 4, quoted in Barker, *Apostasy*, 48.

8. Irenaeus, *Against Heresies*, iv, 7,2, 4, quoted in Barker, *Apostasy*, 48.

9. Mourett, *Histoire Generale de l'Eglise*, vol. 1, 316, quoted in Barker, *Apostasy*, 48.

10. T. Edgar Lyon, *Apostasy to Restoration* (Salt Lake City: Deseret Book, 1960), 232–33.

11. McConkie, *Mormon Doctrine*, 340.

12. Celsus, *On the True Doctrine*, 103, quoted in McConkie, *Sons and Daughters*, 108–9.

13. Joseph Fielding McConkie, *Sons and Daughters of God* (Salt Lake City: Bookcraft, 1994), 109.

14. Barker, *Apostasy*, 229.

15. Alfred Weber, *History of Philosophy*, 84–89, quoted in Barker, *Apostasy*, 230.

16. Jefferson, *Writings*, 1342, quoted in McConkie, *Sons and Daughters*, 147.

17. McConkie, *Sons and Daughters*, 55.

18. Ibid., 7.

SECTION IV
THE REQUIREMENTS
OF SALVATION

Question #10

I have two very close and very religious friends, each one trying to interest me in their church. When I attend one church, I am taught that in the hereafter I will be judged according to my deeds and so I must earn a place in heaven by performing sufficient good works to offset my sins. In my other friend's church, I am told that it is my faith in Christ received through the grace of God that saves me, and that good works are really not necessary in order for me to make it into heaven. I am told that as long as I profess a belief in Jesus Christ, I will automatically be saved—nothing else is required. So, which church is telling me the truth? Am I saved by my good works or am I simply saved by the grace of God alone? I guess what I'm really asking is, what must I do to get to heaven and to receive the blessings of eternal life?

Are we saved by works or saved by grace? This is the subject of great division and disagreement among modern Christian churches. To be quite frank, however, neither of these two conflicting and contradictory beliefs is correct. Is a person saved by his good works alone? No. Is a person saved by the grace of God alone? Again, the answer is no. Later, we will discuss the true requirements of salvation as originally taught by Christ and the early Church leaders. But, for comparison's sake, let us first see what modern Christian churches commonly teach on this matter.

Why, we might ask, is there such a great debate and controversy in the modern Christian world over something so central to the gospel of Jesus Christ as the basic requirements of salvation? Why is Christianity so divided on this matter? To begin to understand, let us go back in time to a period when early Christian doctrines were so greatly changing, evolving, and drifting far off course from original gospel teachings.

PURGATORY, INDULGENCES, AND THE TREASURY OF MERIT

In the very early years of Christianity, Church leaders emphasized the divine origins and potential of man, and the tremendous love that God feels for His children. As centuries passed, however, Christian leaders began instead to promote and emphasize a very negative view of man and God. Man was considered to be a sinful, miserable worm, stained by original sin and worthy only of hellfire and damnation at life's end. Men became so terrified of God's vengeance that many feared to even pray directly to Him, believing that He would not even listen to a prayer uttered from their sinful lips. Thus, many began to pray to intermediary saints instead, requesting that these saints pray to God in their behalf.

As the focus of Christian worship gradually became centered on the sinful nature of man and the need to gain forgiveness, a practice evolved within the medieval Church requiring a church member to confess all of his sins to his priest. In turn, the priest would assign to the confessing sinner the number of good works necessary for him to perform in order to offset his sins and thus gain forgiveness. These good works generally took the form of reciting memorized prayers, fasting, attending worship services, and so forth.

Such good works were not performed out of a feeling of love or grace or a deep desire to serve God and mankind. Rather, they were performed out of a feeling of great fear towards God and towards the terrible punishment that awaited them as sinners. Thus, these acts were self-centered— done strictly for one's own benefit.

In earlier times, a love for God and for all mankind had caused devout Christians to get outside of themselves through acts of humble obedience to God and selfless service to others. Now, possessing a great fear of God and His judgments, Christians turned inward, caring first and foremost about their own eternal welfare. Men were not so concerned about living righteously and qualifying for heaven as they were with obtaining forgiveness for their sins and thus escaping the sufferings of hellfire. By the middle of the fourth century, "salvation had come to emphasize, not how to attain character growth, by the avoidance of sin and by service to the neighbor, but rather how to avoid punishment, the penalty for sin."[1]

In a sense, the medieval church had regressed back to the "lesser law" of ancient Israel wherein obedience to God was motivated by a fear of punishment. The higher law of Christ's gospel, wherein obedience to God is motivated by a person's perfect love for God, was largely abandoned. This extremely negative view of God, man, and salvation would be further distorted by the introduction of even more innovations in doctrine.

> A theory made its appearance about the fourth century representing that the priest at confession could not purge the confessing sinner of all the punishment due for sin. In fact, no amount of penitentials could completely obliterate this, as God reserved for Himself certain punishments after the death of the repentant sinner. The priest at confession could only absolve from those sins which God had not reserved for post-mortal punishment. Augustine [Bishop of Hippo, AD 400— the same who was the originator of the doctrine of original sin] had a doctrine that there was a place where those who were not sufficiently bad to be confined to hell could be punished with God's punishment until they had made atonement for their sins. . . . [Pope] Gregory the Great [AD 600] wrote much about it and developed the idea until it became a fixed part of the belief of most western Christians by the tenth century. The teaching of the church elaborated the awfulness of purgatorial punishment until sincere believers trembled at the thought of the horrors that awaited them, even though they had confessed all of their sins and fulfilled their penance assignments. . . .
>
> The indulgence doctrine evolved as a partial solution to the dilemma.[2]

The granting of indulgences, by which one could pay money to the Church, gain further forgiveness for sins, and thus escape the terrible punishment of purgatory, was given a theological basis by still another new theory called the Treasury of Merit. This doctrine was developed during the twelfth century by an English Franciscan monk, Alexander of Hales. He theorized,

> There actually existed an immense treasure of *merit*, composed of the pious deeds and virtuous actions which the saints had performed *beyond what was necessary for their own salvation*, and which were therefore applicable to the benefit of others; that the guardian and dispenser of this precious treasure was the Roman pontiff [pope], and that of consequence he was empowered to assign to such as he thought proper a portion of this inexhaustible source of merit, suitable to their respective guilt, and sufficient to deliver them from the punishment due to their crimes.[3]

As part of the process of obtaining forgiveness, an individual was still required to confess his sins; but rather than doing penance or good works as assigned by the priest, he simply purchased with his money some of the good works of dead saints, which were stored in the Treasury of Merit in heaven. Church members could also purchase from the priest good works from the Treasury of Merit to offset the sins of their dead relatives who they felt might be experiencing terrible suffering in purgatory. By so doing, they hoped to be able to secure their release and allow them to enter heaven.

These new, man-made doctrines became even more exaggerated and perverted during the sixteenth century when John Tetzel, acting as an agent of the Pope, began selling indulgences in Germany in order to raise money to finish Saint Peter's Cathedral at the Vatican. These very special indulgences, as authorized by Rome, required no confession of sin to a priest, and they could even offset sins that a person had not yet committed but was planning to commit in the future! In essence, someone could live a far less than righteous life and still escape purgatory and be saved in heaven if willing to pay the necessary price in gold and silver to the Church.

If sins could be forgiven by the performance, or even the purchase, of good works, then what need was there for a Savior to offer forgiveness and to redeem mankind?

The Doctrine of Salvation by Grace Alone

Martin Luther and other Protestant Reformers of the sixteenth century recognized that a gross error had crept into the Church. However, rather than return to the original teachings of early Christianity on this matter, these Reformers developed a whole new philosophy concerning the attainment of salvation.

For centuries the Roman Catholic Church had taught that salvation came by having sins forgiven through the performance (or purchase) of good works. In direct opposition to this teaching, the Reformers declared that simply God's grace alone, without the need for the performance of any good works whatsoever, was all that was necessary for salvation.

Like the pendulum of a great clock, the views of so many Christians had now swung from one extreme to the other.

According to Luther, grace did not represent those many free gifts, such as Christ's Atonement for sin, that God had made available and could be obtained by any or all of His children. Rather, grace was something that God had reserved for only a select few.

Luther believed that all men were evil by nature—that they were totally depraved—and thus were only worthy of hellfire and damnation at life's end. However, because of God's merciful nature He had decided to bestow His grace upon a fortunate few. These particularly lucky individuals He would draw to Himself with an irresistible power. Allowing them no freedom to choose for themselves, He would force them to have faith in Christ and thus be worthy of salvation. However, those who were not so lucky as to have been selected by God for this bestowal of grace (which unfortunately constituted the great majority of mankind) would simply be allowed to travel to life's end—and then He would send them off to their well-deserved place in hell.

According to Luther, there was no such thing as free will in man:

> He [Luther] inseparably connects divine foreknowledge and fore-ordination [predestination], and infers from God's almighty power that all things happen by necessity, and that there can be no freedom in the creature. He represents the human will as a horse or as a donkey which goes just as the rider directs it; and that rider is the devil in the state of fallen nature, and God in the state of grace. The will has no choice of master; it is God and the devil who are fighting for its possession. The scripture exhortations to repentance and holy living must not be understood seriously, but ironically, as if God would say to man: "Only try to repent and to do good, and you will find that you cannot do it" (Schaff, *A History of the Christian Church*, vol. 7, 431).[4]

With no personal freedom of will to do good or to repent of one's sins, the final judgment of mankind by God thus becomes a farce. This teaching of Luther, in the opinion of Erasmus (a contemporary Reformer and critic of Luther), is the same as saying, "God works in us good and evil, and crowns His good works in us, and punishes his bad works in us."[5] In other words, God creates a man evil; He then takes away his free will and makes it impossible for him to be otherwise; and finally He holds that man personally responsible and eternally punishes him for being so. Is this a just and fair God?

According to Luther, those who had been selected for salvation by God were virtually forced to heaven. He taught that if a man came to believe that Jesus was his Savior and would confess this truth, he obviously had come under the saving power of God's grace and his salvation was assured, nothing else being required of him.

The Teachings of Other Protestant Reformers

Ulrich Zwingli in Switzerland held views close to Luther's on the matter of salvation by grace alone. However, before he could completely form his views, Zwingli was killed on the battlefield during a war between Catholics and Protestants. Taking his place and finishing his work was the well-known reformer John Calvin.

Concerning free will and salvation, the Protestant historian Schaff summarizes Calvin's teachings as follows:

> God has from eternity foreordained [predestined] all things that will come to pass, with a view to the manifestation of His glory; He created man pure and holy, and with freedom of choice; Adam was tried, disobeyed, lost his freedom, and became a slave of sin; the whole human race fell with him, and is justly condemned in Adam to everlasting death; but God in his sovereign mercy elects part of this mass of corruption to everlasting life, *without regard to moral merit*, converts the elect by *irresistible* grace, justifies, sanctifies, and perfects them, and thus displays in them the riches of His grace; while in His inscrutable, yet just and adorable counsel, He leaves the rest of mankind in their inherited state of condemnation, and reveals in the everlasting punishment of the wicked the glory of his awful justice.[6]

According to Calvin, God had predestined each man and woman to either salvation or damnation before they ever came into existence. God had predetermined and had virtually scripted every action they would ever perform, making each person much like an actor in a play. There was no possibility for a person to change or influence his or her ultimate destiny. Although Calvin and the many other early Reformers who taught the doctrines of human depravity and predestination would carefully avoid declaring that God was the author of sin and the source of all evil as well as all good, a logical analysis of their teachings could lead to no other conclusion.

Calvin's teachings would form the basis of belief for the many Reformed Churches of the nations of continental Europe, the Anglican Churches, and the Presbyterian and Episcopal Churches in America. In England, King Henry VIII instigated a break with Rome that led to the rise of the the Church of England, which ultimately accepted Calvin's teachings:

> Henry VIII had criticized Luther's *Babylonian Captivity*; and had been given the title, Defender of the Faith, by the pope. In doctrine he was Catholic. . . .

The immediate occasion for the breach with Rome was the king's desire to marry Anne Boleyn. For eighteen years, Henry had been married to Catherine of Aragon. Of this marriage, one child, Mary, survived. Henry sought to have his marriage with Catherine declared invalid by the pope.[7]

When the pope refused Henry's petition, the king broke ties with Rome and declared himself the head of the Church in England.

The church under Henry VIII, remained Catholic in doctrine. . . . Rebellious Protestants, who refused to subscribe to the Catholic doctrines, were condemned to the stake; and rebellious Catholics, who refused to accept the king as head of the church, were condemned to the gallows. "Accordingly, on July 30, 1543, the strange sight was seen in Smithfield of six simultaneous executions, three burnings for heresy and three hangings for denial of the royal headship of the Church" (Clarke, *Short History of the Christian Church*, p. 288.). . . .

On the death of Henry VIII, in 1547, the ten-year-old son of Henry VIII and Jane Seymour became king of England. . . . Under Edward VI, the country moved successively towards Protestantism . . . and a Lutheran liturgy was adopted. . . .

After a short reign (1547–1553), Edward VI was succeeded by Mary Tudor . . . [whose] fervent Catholicism, led her to restore Catholicism. Old laws condemning heretics to the stake were enforced and two hundred eighty were burned. The severity of "bloody Mary" did much to turn public sentiment to Protestantism though it too had been, and was to be, intolerant [of all other churches]. . . .

Elizabeth, the daughter of Henry VIII and Anne Boleyn, succeeded Mary. The queen was perhaps Catholic in sentiment, but the pope had declared her mother's marriage illegal and had excommunicated her father. If Elizabeth were illegitimate, she had no legal claim to the throne.

Naturally Elizabeth turned to Protestantism. And, like her father, she was determined to have supreme authority in church as well as state. Parliament again voted the Act of Supremacy, declaring her to be the Supreme Regulator of the Church, and the Act of Uniformity to oblige all to follow the *Book of Common Prayer*, thus restoring the Calvinistic worship of the reign of Edward VI.[8]

Compare the birth of this church, which came about through the whims and designs of earthly kings, with that of Christ's both ancient and restored church, which came about through the designs of heavenly

Kings. There is quite a difference between the origin of a human church and that of a divine church, to say the least.

The later reformer John Wesley (1703–1791), like his father before him, was an ordained minister in the Church of England. Wesley's studies, however, led him to a break with many of the Calvinistic teachings of the Church, which ultimately led to the establishment of the Methodist Church.

> His [Wesley's] history covers almost the whole of the eighteenth century, and his importance goes beyond a narrow definition of organized religion and more broadly to education and literature, prisons and poverty.
>
> Wesley's desire to do good gave him great energy. He traveled approximately five thousand miles on foot or horseback each year. He generally preached fifteen sermons a week. He wrote over four hundred publications and aided his brother in the compilation of some six thousand hymns. With the help of his sister he made good books available at low prices. The two wrote books of their own and rewrote others in easier diction so that people of limited education could read them. Wesley's concern for the poor put him far in advance of his time in social reform. He supplied the poor with clothes and food and helped make arrangements for the satisfying of their debts. He established a lending fund to help struggling businesses. He opened dispensaries in London and Bristol and was often the only medic the poor ever saw. In all these actions, Wesley felt that he was "called of God."
>
> Because of his public activities, however, he was viewed as a threat to ministers of the gospel who collected their fees and spent their time hunting and fishing. Wesley's promotion of the value of human souls was seen as politically incorrect. As early as 1732 he was decried in the press, and not more than five years later his character was publicly slandered and attacked in court.
>
> Of these experiences Wesley, said: "All crimes have been laid to my charge of which a human being is capable, except drunkenness." Wesley had no sooner uttered these words when a ragged wretch jumped up, exclaiming that Wesley had made a trade with a lady friend of hers for a considerable amount of whisky. Having made her case she sat down amid a thunderstruck assembly. Mr. Wesley, unmoved, merely "thanked God that his cup was now full."[9]

Unlike Calvin, Wesley[10] believed that God had given men and women freedom of will—that a person could come to accept Christ as their Savior without being forced by God to do so. Calvinism taught that

God had predestined each person to either salvation or damnation before they had even been born. An individual who had been granted grace by God could not fall from grace. Wesley, on the other hand, believed that a man who chose to accept Christ and receive the grace of God could later fall from grace and still later regain grace. He was regularly denounced and persecuted for these and other teachings that opposed Calvinistic doctrines. For example, "At a conference in 1770, he drew a rebuke from rigid Calvinists by presenting resolutions which stated that the heathen who had never heard of Christ could be saved if they feared God and lived up to such light as they had."[11]

Although Luther, Calvin, Wesley, and other Protestant Reformers disagreed on many points of doctrine, such as free will, exclusivism, and scores of others, most of them (although not all) did agree on one basic issue: that salvation came through faith and grace, and that the performance of good works by an individual was not necessary or required in the attainment of salvation. They emphasized the fact that salvation was a gift from God that could not be earned simply by good works alone (which is true), but they failed to recognize the fact that an individual was still required to merit or qualify for salvation—that indeed Christ was "the author of eternal salvation unto all them that *obey* him" (Hebrews 5:9; italics added).

The doctrine of salvation by grace alone, commonly preached by most of the Reformers for over four hundred years now, has had a terribly negative affect on the lives of so many individuals. Let me give you an example of what I mean.

Many years ago while serving as a young missionary in the wonderful land of Australia, I one day met a man with whom I had the privilege of discussing religion. He was a member of a large and popular Protestant sect of our day, and in talking with him it soon became evident he was not the least bit interested in hearing anything I had to say concerning the restored gospel of Jesus Christ. As he explained to me, he had been "saved" and was in need of no further knowledge concerning the matter. His certainty in this conviction fascinated me, and I desired to learn more about it.

With great interest I listened as he told me of his moment of "salvation"—the moment he had confessed Christ as his Savior—which he was able to pinpoint in time to the exact hour and even minute. My curiosity aroused by this, I questioned him on how he could be so certain that he would be saved in heaven with many years possibly left in his life, during which time he might fall into major transgression and sin or live a life less than worthy to stand in God's presence. He informed me that no action on his part, whether for good or evil, had any bearing on this. The fact that he had accepted Christ as his Savior was the only requirement necessary for salvation.

My curiosity aroused even more by this last statement, I posed a hypothetical question to him: "What if you were to go next door tomorrow and murder your neighbor, deliberately and in cold blood . . . would you still be saved?" Without a moment's hesitation, he emphatically declared, "Yes!"

As you can imagine, I was quite astonished by his reply. Now I know that it is highly unlikely that this particular individual would ever think to actually murder someone during his lifetime. But what really concerned me was the feeling I received from him that he believed he could live any type of life he desired—righteous, lukewarm, or actually evil. He was absolutely convinced that as long as he professed a belief in Christ, he could be totally certain of his salvation whether he were obedient or totally disobedient to God's laws and commandments.

Equally sad and disturbing to me was the fact that his belief in this unreasonable and untrue doctrine had completely blinded him and had closed his mind. He was totally unwilling to listen even for a moment to the truths of Christ's restored gospel that I had traveled all the way to Australia to give him.

This doctrine of salvation by grace alone continues to be extremely popular among millions of people even today (but obviously only among those who believe that they themselves are among the chosen, saved few). And, of course, why wouldn't it be popular? How very easy is the path back to God—all you have to do is confess with your lips that Jesus is the Christ. You can then lie back against a tree, dream of your future mansion in heaven, and do little or nothing as you please!

It is not difficult to see why modern counterfeits to Christ's original teachings have become so popular among mankind, for both of these man-made doctrines we have just discussed teach us that it is so easy to get to heaven. The doctrine of indulgences, as practiced for hundreds of years during medieval times, taught that total obedience to God's commandments was not really necessary, since the good works of others could be used to offset one's own personal deficiencies. If you were a little wicked, it was all right—you could still buy your way into heaven by paying money to your priest. On the other hand, the more modern doctrine of salvation by grace alone provides an even easier way to get to heaven. It teaches a man that no work or effort at all is required on his part. For if he happens to get lucky and is randomly elected for salvation by some divine whim of God, God Himself will do all the work that is needed for him to be saved. Once again, you only need to have faith—you don't need to be faithful.

Both of these theories convey basically the same message to the mind of man. They both teach that it is not really necessary for you to personally put forth your best effort at living the commandments of God in order to reap salvation, because somebody else already has done, or will do, all of the work for you! As we will see in the next section, how very different are these teachings from the original teachings of Christ. And how extremely blessed we are to have the original teachings of the Savior on these matters once more restored to earth in our day.

QUESTION #11

What must I do to be allowed to enter the presence of God in the highest of heavens and to receive the blessings of eternal life? In other words, what must I do to be saved?

In the previous section, we noted that some modern Christian churches teach that a man is saved by his good works. Many other churches teach the opposite—that man is saved by the grace of God alone, without the need of performing any good works. We then learned that, actually, *neither* of these explanations is correct. Let us now discuss what is really required for you and me to qualify for salvation and the gift of eternal life.

THE THREE REQUIREMENTS OF SALVATION

During the early years of Christianity, it was taught that there were three basic requirements, each of which had to be met, in order for a person to qualify for eternal life in the presence of God. These were (1) to have faith in the Lord Jesus Christ, (2) to perform good works, and (3) to receive the grace of God. Let me emphasize again that each one of these was required—not one of them could be eliminated or disregarded. Let us take a moment to examine each one of these requirements more closely.

Faith in Jesus Christ

Earlier I quoted a statement of the Savior that merits both repeating and emphasis. Christ clearly taught, "I am the way, the truth, and the life: no man cometh unto the Father, but by me" (John 14:6). Why do we need

Christ to act as our Savior in order for us to enter God's presence? Because, as the apostle Paul declared, all of us are sinners, "for all have sinned, and come short of the glory of God" (Romans 3:23). Because our sins make us unclean, every one of us is unworthy to enter God's presence.

Because our Heavenly Father is a perfectly just Being, He requires that a punishment be given for every sin we commit. Every commandment that is broken by any one of His children requires that a price be paid. However, because He is also a perfectly loving and merciful Father, He does not want to punish any of His children if they are truly sorry for their mistakes and humbly seek His forgiveness.

So how can God be both perfectly just and perfectly merciful at the same time? These two divine attributes seem to contradict one another. In the wisdom of God, He knew that in order for His justice to be satisfied, and at the same time His mercy extended, it would require the work of a mediator—one individual standing between Him and His children to act as a Savior.

Because of His infinite love for us, and in order to satisfy the demands of God's justice, Christ volunteered to take upon Himself the punishment that God requires for sin. As the mediator, Christ, a perfect and sinless Being, stood between God and man and suffered for our sins so we would not have to suffer. Only a sinless Being could do this—His suffering was for *our* sins only, because He had none of His own for which to be punished. In the Garden of Gethsemane, Christ's suffering for our sins was so great that He sweat great drops of blood. In His agony on the cross, He sacrificed His very life for each one of us. "The blood of Jesus Christ . . . cleanseth us from all sin. If we say that we have no sin, we deceive ourselves, and the truth is not in us. If we confess our sins, he is faithful and just to forgive us our sins, and to cleanse us from all unrighteousness" (1 John 1:7–9).

This sacrifice made by the Lord on our behalf only takes effect in our lives if we recognize and accept Him as our Savior, humbly repent of our sins, and actively seek to do God's will. As we do this, Christ removes our sins from us, and we do not have to suffer for them in the hereafter, for He has already suffered the required punishment in our place.

Thus, through Christ, God's justice is served, for sin has been punished; but at the same time God's mercy has been extended, for we do not have to suffer for our sins if we truly, humbly repent. However, if we do not look to the Savior and humbly repent of our sins, then in the pure justice of God, we will have to bear the punishment for our own sins in the life yet to come.

God has informed us that no unclean thing can dwell in His presence, and we can only become clean and free from the stains of sin through Christ. It is obvious that faith in Christ and an acceptance of Him as our personal Savior are absolutely essential if we ever hope to return to God's presence.

The Good Works of Man

As used in the scriptures, the term *good works* refers to (1) obedience to the laws and commandments of God, and (2) unselfish, loving service to mankind. These are acts that characterized the Savior's life; His was a life of total obedience to God and boundless love and service to mankind. As disciples of Christ, we are expected to follow His perfect example.

Good works naturally flow from an individual who has gained a true and living faith in the Savior. Among those who profess to have faith in Christ but do not perform the good works that flow from such faith, obviously their faith is "dead" (see James 2:14–20)—that is, it is not a true and living faith and cannot bring them eternal life.

All scriptural references to the final judgment of God indicate the basis of that judgment will be the works of men—that is, what their deeds have actually been, whether good or evil.

We find ample evidence of this in the Bible: "And I saw the dead, small and great, stand before God; and the books were opened: and another book was opened, which is the book of life: and the dead were judged out of those things which were written in the books, *according to their works*. And the sea gave up the dead which were in it; and death and hell delivered up the dead which were in them: and they were judged every man *according to their works*" (Revelation 20:12–13; italics added).

In Romans we read, "But after thy hardness and impenitent heart treasurest up unto thyself wrath against the day of wrath and revelation of the righteous judgment of God; Who will render to every man *according to his deeds*" (Romans 2:5–6, 13; italics added). It is not the *hearers* of the law who are just before God, but the *doers* of the law.

Matthew writes, "For the Son of man will come in the glory of his Father with his angels; and then he will reward every man *according to his works*" (Matthew 16:27; italics added).

As men and women stand before Christ to be judged, He will look to their deeds of righteousness or wickedness to determine the reward they will receive. Among those who profess to believe in Christ, He will look to their works of obedience and love to verify that such faith really exists. Obviously, the empty and unsubstantiated pronouncements of faith that proceed from their lips will be meaningless to Him. For as the Savior Himself has indicated, "Not every one that *saith* unto me, Lord, Lord, will enter into the kingdom of heaven; but he that *doeth* the will of my Father which is in heaven" (Matthew 7:21; italics added).

Thus, to qualify for the highest of heavens one must have more than just faith—he or she must be faithful.

The Grace of God

Even though a man has great faith in Christ and, as a result of such faith, strives to live in strict obedience to the commandments of God, this alone is not sufficient to save him. Ultimately, it is through the grace of God that a man will one day be allowed to dwell in His divine presence. A modern-day apostle gives us the following definition of grace: "*God's grace* consists in his love, mercy, and condescension toward his children. All things that exist are manifestations of the grace of God. The creation of the earth, life itself, the atonement of Christ, the plan of salvation, kingdoms of immortal glory hereafter, and the supreme gift of eternal life—all these things come by the grace of him whose we are."[12]

Thus, grace represents God's love. Because He loves us so much He gives us certain gifts, and without such gifts it would be impossible to return to Him. For example, He gave us the gift of life. He gave us the gift of a physical body—something we certainly could not provide for ourselves. Because of His love for us, the Savior gave us the gift of the Atonement, suffering for our sins so we would not have to suffer. He gave us the gift of one day having a perfect, immortal, resurrected body. He provides us with the gift of the Holy Ghost to help us perfect ourselves. These all come to us as gifts from God. Obviously, without the many gifts that God freely showers upon us through His love, goodness, or grace, we could never hope to gain the gift of eternal life.

THE GIFT OF THE HOLY GHOST: A MANIFESTATION OF GOD'S GRACE

Grace is defined, in part, as "an enabling power" or a "divine means of help or strength, given through the bounteous mercy and love of Jesus Christ."[13] So just what is this "enabling power" or additional strength that is bestowed upon us through the grace of God, without which we would be unable to return to His presence? It is the power of God. This power is most commonly manifest to mankind through the gift and power of the Holy Ghost.

When the Savior was upon the earth, He taught His disciples that unless they were "born of water and of the spirit" (John 3:5) they could not enter into the kingdom of heaven. While being "born of water" is accomplished through baptism, being "born of the spirit" is accomplished through the receipt of the Holy Ghost.

The Holy Ghost, or Holy Spirit, is the third member of the Godhead, a divine personage of spirit whose influence the Savior promised to send His disciples shortly after His departure. (See John 16:7, 13.) The Holy Ghost fulfills a number of assignments, some of which include revealing truth to the heart and mind of those who actively seek it; bringing peace to those in need of comfort; testifying of the divinity of the Lord Jesus Christ; and endowing worthy men and women with the gifts of the spirit. These gifts include such blessings as the gift of discernment, the gift of faith, the gift of wisdom, the gift of charity (pure love), the gift of healing, gifts of prophecy and revelation, and the gift of tongues (languages) and the interpretation of tongues. One cannot help but see, from this list, what a great blessing it would be for any person to have the influence of this divine Spirit in his life.

As a revelator, the Holy Ghost will confirm the truth within the hearts of those who are seeking it. For example, in the New Testament account, those listening to the preaching of Peter and the other apostles on the day of Pentecost were "pricked in their heart" (Acts 2:37)—meaning they were touched by the influence of this divine Spirit, whereby they knew that what they were being taught was true. With a newly acquired faith in the divinity of Christ, they asked Peter and the others, "Men and brethren, what will we do? Then Peter said unto them, *Repent*, and *be baptized* every one of you in the name of Jesus Christ for the remission of sins, and ye will *receive the gift of the Holy Ghost*" (Acts 2:37–38; italics added).

Faith, repentance, baptism, the gift of the Holy Ghost—as the scriptures indicate, these are the basic principles and ordinances of the gospel of Jesus Christ that start us on our journey back to God. All three elements of salvation are represented here. We begin by acquiring a faith in Jesus Christ. But faith alone is not sufficient to save us. We must actually *do* something—some works that manifest our faith: we must repent and be baptized. Following our baptism, we then are blessed with a manifestation of God's grace: we are given the gift of the Holy Ghost.

As this story teaches us, although these people were "pricked in their heart"—meaning they were touched by the influence of the Holy Ghost—Peter taught that they would not receive the gift of the Holy Ghost until *after* they had been baptized. For though the influence of this divine Spirit will come, revealing and testifying of truth to those who are humbly and sincerely seeking it, it will not linger with those who do not act upon its promptings. To such individuals, this divine influence will come, and then it will depart.

The gift of the Holy Ghost spoken of by Peter is a blessing—a manifestation of God's grace—that is reserved only for those who heed the Spirit's direction and enter the Lord's church through baptism. This gift, which is given to a person after baptism, is the right and privilege to have the constant companionship of this member of the Godhead in their life—predicated, of course, upon their continued worthiness to have this divine influence with them.

At the time of baptism, our former sins are remitted and washed from us through the blood of Christ, and we, for the moment, stand perfectly clean before God. But even though clean, our very nature and character remains far from perfect. Becoming "born again," or born of the Spirit, is not simply a one-time event that takes place at the time of our baptism or our acceptance of Christ as our Savior. Faith, repentance, and baptism open the gate to the strait and narrow path leading to eternal life—but there is a long road ahead of us. Baptism begins the process by which a gradual spiritual transformation takes place within our heart and mind. Our goal is ultimately, over time, to become a "new creature" in Christ (2 Corinthians 5:17).

This change of our nature and character is brought about by the Holy Ghost. Through the regenerating and sanctifying power of the Holy Ghost, not only can a person's sins be removed, but his very *desire* to sin can be removed. As this process continues—as he moves forward on the path—he will come to fully and freely surrender his own will unto the will of Christ and the Father, even as Christ surrendered His will unto the will of the Father. Even as Christ is one with the Father, we will become one with Christ and the Father.

Such transformed individuals are totally devoted to Christ. They gradually come to think like He thinks, to desire what He desires, and to act like He acts—in other words, they become like Him. This perfecting and transforming process will not be totally complete until sometime in the next life, at which time we will be fully prepared to enter the Father's presence and receive the gift of eternal life.

What a tremendous blessing it is to enjoy the actual presence of one of the members of the Godhead in our lives. The Holy Ghost acts as a comforter, a guide, and a tutor for us. Although today we are unprepared and unworthy to stand in the Father's presence, the workings of the Spirit within us help to prepare us, cleanse us, sanctify us, and make us worthy to enter His divine presence. As we exercise discipline and self-control, the Spirit greatly magnifies our own efforts as we move forward on the path towards perfection. Although we must continually put forth our own best effort, we cannot accomplish this total transformation on our own or simply through our own efforts or works. Only with the help of this third member of the Godhead, provided to us as an act of grace or love from Christ, can we eventually become worthy and prepared to stand before God.

Other Characteristics of Grace

One LDS writer provides us with some important insights into the nature of God's grace:

> Grace may be defined as an unmerited gift or endowment given as a manifestation of divine love and compassion, for which the recipient does not pay an equivalent price. But though grace is unearned, it need not be unmerited. When Jesus received the attributes and powers of His Father's glory, He received grace *for* grace; that is, He received divine endowments of the Father's glory as He gave grace to others. Service and dedication to the welfare of others, in doing the will of the Father, therefore were keystone principles in Christ's spiritual development.[14]

Yes, even our Savior, Jesus Christ, received grace from the Father—that is, gifts or endowments of strength, power, and ultimately exaltation and all things that God has. He received these manifestations of the Father's love or grace as He humbly and fully complied with the will of the Father and bestowed grace or love upon others. (See John 1:16; D&C 93:11–14.) Indeed, He received "grace for grace"—that is, He received grace from the Father as He gave grace to God's children.

We are told in the scriptures that both the Father and the Son are divine Beings who are full of grace, or love. They manifest this grace or love for mankind by providing us with "gifts." In order for something to be a gift, it must be unearned. For example, when a father gives a gift to his child on his birthday, it is not in payment for any work that the child has done, but is simply a manifestation of the love the father feels for his child. He wants his child to be happy. Similarly, Christ provided His Atonement for sin as a gift to all mankind, and He spent His life in mortality blessing and serving countless individuals as well—not in payment for service He had received from them, but simply because He loves them and He wants them to be happy.

Christ came to earth not only to fulfill His work of performing the required infinite Atonement for sin, but also to show us, by His perfect example, what we must become in order to one day dwell in the Father's presence. To stand in God's presence, we must eventually become "like him" (1 John 3:2). What is God like and how can we become like Him? We can learn what God is like by studying the life of Christ—for in every way, Christ is just like His, and our, Father. How can we become perfect like the Father? By becoming perfect like Christ. As we study the life, nature, attributes, and teachings of Christ, we can learn exactly what we can and will be like one day, if we but follow His perfect example and do what He asks us to do.

Just as Christ received "grace for grace" from the Father, so can we. (See D&C 93:20.) Just as Christ gave His grace or love to others, so must we. In doing so, we become like Christ, and thus like the Father. So how do we manifest our love or grace to others? Just like Christ did—by serving others.

For example, when a person gives service in the Church by teaching a Sunday School class, he is manifesting his grace for members of that class. He is willing to sacrifice a number of hours of his personal time in preparing and teaching the lesson, not as payment for anything that members of the class may have done for him, but simply because he loves them and cares about their eternal welfare. He is giving them a gift of his time, talents, and effort—a gift of grace.

When we give service or money to help the poor, we are similarly manifesting our grace. Our gift of time or money is not given to repay what we have received from these less fortunate souls, but is simply our way of showing our love and concern for the temporal as well as spiritual welfare of others. So also, when young missionaries leave home and family to serve in the mission field for two years, their selfless service and personal sacrifice is a manifestation of grace, or the deep love they feel for God and their fellow man. In providing this service, there is no thought of personal, worldly gain on their part. Nevertheless, as they are both obedient to God's commandments and give grace, they in turn receive grace; and those who faithfully serve typically return home greatly changed individuals—much further along the strait and narrow pathway to perfection and eternal life than they had been two years earlier.

Of course there are countless ways to offer the gift of grace or love to others—not just through church service, but through service at home, in our neighborhood, and in our community or country as well. When we offer our grace to others, God in turn bestows upon us grace by blessing us with an additional outpouring of the gift of the Holy Ghost, through which we become sanctified and increase the perfection of our character, thus becoming more like the Savior. This truly is a gift from the Father and the Son, not simply a payment for our service or good works—for God's blessings to us are always far greater in value and volume than are the blessings that we are able to offer others. Figuratively speaking, we give one piece of silver to others, and God gives five pieces of gold to us. Try as we might, we cannot out-give God. We are, and forever will be, in debt to Him.

There are many gifts that God makes available to all of His children through His grace, such as the gift of the resurrection. All mankind, both those who are righteous and those who are wicked, will receive this gift. There are many other gifts that God gives to His children, however, that although unearned, must nevertheless be merited. That may sound confusing or contradictory. But take for example the gift of the Holy Ghost. This is indeed a gift or manifestation of God's grace, but it is not automatically bestowed upon all of God's children. Certain prerequisites must be met before one can receive it: a person must first have faith in the Savior, repent of his sins, and then enter the Lord's church through baptism. Then the gift is given. Similarly, during His mortal mission, before Christ would bestow His healing gift upon a sick or disabled person, usually they (or a relative of theirs) would first have to indicate their faith in Him and in His ability to heal them. Although this gift (healing) was unearned, it nonetheless had to be sought and merited.

Now, there are many gifts that God bestows upon His children, but none is greater than the gift of eternal life. Yes, throughout the scriptures eternal life is always spoken of as a gift from God, something that our good works or personal effort cannot really *earn*. For as the apostle Paul notes, "The gift of God is eternal life through Jesus Christ our Lord" (Romans 6:23). Like so many of God's other gifts, eternal life is something that is not earned, but nevertheless must be sought after and merited. If this concept still seems somewhat contradictory or confusing to you, perhaps a little story or parable will help illustrate what I mean by all this.

A Boy Learns the Meaning of Faith, Works, and Grace

There was once a very rich and powerful ruler who had five sons. His eldest son was far wiser than the others, and so the father made him overseer over all his lands and possessions. One day the ruler gave instructions to his four younger sons to go out to the fields, for there was some very important work to do. They were told that when they arrived at a certain field, their older brother would be there to explain exactly what needed to be done. Before they left, the boys were told if they accomplished what was asked of them that day, they would receive a wonderful gift.

Upon arriving at the designated spot, they found their elder brother waiting. He explained to the boys that four irrigation ditches needed to be constructed that day to irrigate four fields the following day. The eldest son had already outlined on the surface of the ground a strait and narrow pathway for each of the boys to follow. They each had eight hours before sunset to dig a ditch three feet wide, one foot deep, and eighty feet long.

While digging, they were to be careful to stay within the straight lines that had been drawn on the surface of the ground for them. The older brother said that he would stay close by and come check on the boys from time to time and help them if they were having troubles—all they would have to do is ask him. Each boy was then handed a shovel and began to work.

After tossing a little dirt from his assigned pathway, the first boy heard some of his friends calling out to him and inviting him to come with them to town. At first he declined, for he had work to do. He kept shoveling for a short while more, but eventually he dropped his shovel and traveled with them to town, spending the remainder of the day having fun with his friends.

Halfway through the day, after about four hours or so of digging his assigned ditch, the second boy sat down by a nearby tree to rest and began to think about how wonderful his father and older brother were. He loved both of them so very much. He wondered what wonderful gift his father would be giving him. He could hardly wait to get back home and find out. He didn't worry much about finishing the ditch. After all, he was certain that because his older brother loved him so very much, he would be back to take care of that for him. He then spent the remainder of the day dreaming of the wonderful gift his loving father would give him.

The third boy began working hard to dig the ditch he had been assigned. By mid-afternoon the sun was high in the sky, and it was getting very hot outside. The boy had come to a difficult section that was full of rocks. As he gazed down the pathway ahead of him, he saw he still had a long way to go. The boy determined there was no way that he could finish this job on his own. So he decided to hire some help. He went to town and found some workers, paid them in advance with money he had been carrying in his wallet, and then brought them out to the field and set them to work. How smart he was! Others could do all of the work for him, and he could still finish his assigned task and earn his reward. Like his other brother, he then sat down by a tree near the ditch and spent the remainder of the day lazily thinking about the wonderful gift he would receive from his father.

Like the other boys, the fourth boy also loved his father and older brother very much. But unlike the other boys, he wanted to prove to his father and older brother how much he loved them by doing exactly what they had asked him to do. It was not easy work, but his desire to please those he loved kept him motivated and moving forward. His work was far from perfect. At times he would carelessly make a mistake and dig outside the lines of the marked pathway. He felt terrible about these foolish errors. Whenever he made these mistakes, however, he would call out to his older brother, who was never out of ear's reach. When he did, his older brother always came quickly to his aid and helped him repair the damage he had done. As the hot day wore on, his older brother was there to provide him with food and drink, which refreshed him and helped him regain his strength to keep going. At the end of the day, before the setting of the sun, with the help of his older brother's guidance and encouragement, he had arrived at the end of the path and had successfully completed his assignment.

Early the next morning, the four boys gathered in the living room of their father's mansion, each eagerly anticipating the gift he would receive. Suddenly, their older brother strode into the room and handed each boy an envelope containing a card.

When the first boy, the one who had gone to town with his friends, opened his envelope, he found a handwritten note from his father telling him he was very disappointed with his actions from the previous day. Because of his slothfulness, the boy would be required to spend the remainder of the day with the groundskeepers, pulling weeds in the garden. Nevertheless, he also wanted his son to know that he loved him very much. He was told that later that day, following the completion of his garden assignment, he would be given a five-hundred-dollar bill, payment for the work he had done the previous day in the field.

The boy was sad to receive the reprimand and punishment from his father, although he knew that it was well deserved. He was, however, happy to know his father continued to love him in spite of his foolish actions. He thought back to the day before; he had spent nearly the entire day carousing with his friends. He realized that five hundred dollars was obviously much more than he actually deserved for moving just a few shovelfuls of dirt, and he wondered if he had worked harder if he would have received an even greater payment for his efforts. The answer to his question would soon arrive . . .

The second and third boys, both of whom had spent much of the previous day lazily daydreaming beneath a tree, next opened their envelopes. Both found a note from their father expressing his deep love for them. He said that he was greatly disappointed, however, that they had not fully completed their assigned tasks. Each found a check for four thousand dollars in payment for the work they had done. For their four hours of actual labor in the field, their elder brother informed the boys that they had really only earned forty dollars; but because their father was so very generous and kind, he had actually paid them far more than their efforts deserved. And no, the one boy would not be paid for the work that his hired help had completed—only for his own labors.

Finally, the fourth boy began to open his envelope. He knew that he had worked at least twice as long and hard as his brothers who had just received four thousand dollars. For his faithful efforts, he wondered if his father might actually give him twice as much! Reason and logic, however, told him that he surely hadn't earned that much for his one day of labor. And it really didn't matter anyway. He would be happy just to know that his father was pleased with his efforts and truly loved him. Slowly opening the card, he found a long letter tucked inside, in which his father told of his utmost love and affection for him. Then, behind the letter, he found a check—not for several thousand dollars but for eighty million dollars! And behind this check he found a deed made out in his name for a huge mansion and ten thousand acres of land, which he knew to be located just adjacent to his father's own immense, multi-million-acre estate.

Awestruck, the boy fell to his knees. Looking up at his older brother smiling down at him, he asked how this could be. Surely this could not be payment for his mere one day of labor in the field. "No," the elder brother responded, "you did not *earn* this. This is not payment for your labors. A fair payment for your actual labors would be perhaps eighty dollars. You will never be able to boast and say to your friends that your hard work earned you this reward. No, what you have done is to *qualify* for an inheritance. Because you have proven totally faithful and have been obedient to what your father asked of you, he has given you this gift. It has been given to you because of your father's goodness and grace, or total love for you. Enjoy this gift well."

The previous day, the boy had trusted in his father's word and had felt great hope he would be receiving a marvelous gift from his father if he did what was asked of him. He similarly had great faith in his older brother's word that he would remain nearby to help him with the assigned task. And yet, even though the boy had shown faith and through his own efforts had worked hard to fulfill the assignment, he now realized that without his father's grace, or loving kindness, towards him, he would never have been given a chance to receive such a magnificent inheritance. In fact, he would not have even been born were it not for the grace and love contained in his father's wonderful nature and character.

As he further pondered over what he had just been given, the boy realized that without his older brother's help, he never could have qualified for any of this. It was his older brother who clearly outlined the pathway for him, and who helped him correct and overcome the foolish errors he made along the way. It was his brother who provided the food and drink that gave him the extra strength he needed when his strength began to falter. It was this brother who encouraged him to finish the assigned task, lifting his spirits whenever he felt discouraged. Without the grace or love of his older brother, providing him with help all along the way, the boy knew he could never have made it to the end of the path and thus qualified for this magnificent inheritance.

The gate we each must pass through to enter onto the strait and narrow path, and also into God's earthly kingdom or church, is repentance and baptism by immersion for the remission of sins. The spiritual food and drink provided by Christ through His grace for us, which strengthens us and enables us to continue moving forward on the path, is the gift of the Holy Ghost. There are, of course, many voices heard in the physical world and felt from the unseen world, constantly attempting to lure us off the path, or trying to prevent us from ever finding or starting on the path in the first place. To one day enjoy the gift of eternal life, we must overcome these temptations and distractions, and make our way past the many rocks and stumbling-blocks that are strewn before, beside, and sometimes even on the pathway.

Many modern-day Christian churches teach that God does not actually require people to put forth any effort to move forward on the path— that they can sit idly under a tree and simply profess a belief in Christ and that this alone will save them. During certain periods of history, many others have believed they could actually purchase the good works of dead saints with their money and that these works, performed previously by others, would save them. But the truth is God requires us to exert our best efforts and to endure to the end—that is, once we have entered onto it, we must constantly press forward on the pathway to perfection.

THE GREATEST OF GOD'S GIFTS—ETERNAL LIFE

Of course, far, far greater in value than the eighty million dollars from our little story (indeed, far greater than anything our mortal minds can conceive of) is the gift of eternal life, which God bestows upon His truly valiant, faithful children—those who have endured to the end on the strait and narrow path. Remember that eternal life is always described in the scriptures as a gift. Were a man to live a hundred lifetimes, he could not accumulate sufficient good works to earn this gift or reward. We do not *earn* the gift of eternal life simply through our good works. Rather, we *qualify* ourselves for it through our faith in Christ and through our love for God and all mankind as manifest by the obedience and service we give, being divinely aided in our efforts through the blessings of His grace.

In the simplest of terms, salvation comes to us through the grace or love of God (as manifest through the many gifts that He showers upon us), and through the grace or love we have for God and others (as manifest through our obedience to God and service to our fellow man). It requires God's work and our work; God's gifts and our gifts; God's love and our love; God's grace and our grace.

In the final analysis, eternal life is an inheritance that God bestows upon His most faithful children, a gift freely given because of His grace—a manifestation of His incomprehensible love for us.

Becoming Full of Grace and Truth

The scriptures teach us that Christ is a divine Being "full of grace and truth" (John 1:14, 17; Moses 1:6, 32). To return to God's presence, we too must become individuals who are full of grace and truth. Our grace or love for God is demonstrated by our obedience to Him—for as the Savior Himself instructed His followers, "If ye love me, keep my commandments" (John 14:15). Those who do not keep God's commandments obviously do not love Him. Are such to be blessed and rewarded for their disobedience and lack of grace and love? Of course not. Similarly, we demonstrate our grace and love for others by our concern for the temporal and spiritual welfare of others—by giving selfless service to them. Grace is the giving of the gift of our time, talents, and possessions to bless and lift the lives of others, which we are desirous to do because we love them.

If today we are selfish, tomorrow we can become selfless as we seek and allow the Holy Ghost to transform our natures and our very lives. To become like diety, and thus be worthy to live in God's presence, besides possessing grace, we must also cast aside all false doctrines, false religions, false theories, and false philosophies of men, and be filled with pure, undefiled truth. Only when we ourselves eventually become full of grace and truth, like the Savior is, will we be capable, allowed, and *invited* to walk back to the presence of the Father and His Son. There we will live eternally with Them and with those others we love so dearly who have similarly qualified themselves for this magnificent honor, gift, and inheritance.

Faith in Jesus Christ, the good works of man, and the grace of God—these are the three basic principles leading to salvation or an eternal inheritance in the highest of heavens as originally taught in the earliest years of Christianity. (See 2 Nephi 25:23.) These same original requirements have been revealed to mankind in our day through the Prophet Joseph Smith. It is a simple formula for salvation—a formula that has largely been lost from the knowledge of the modern Christian world. With so much confusion on this matter existing in the world today, how extremely blessed we are to have the *original* teachings of Christ once again so clearly being taught in the Lord's restored church.

NOTES

1. Barker, *Apostasy*, 547.
2. T. Edgar Lyon, *Apostasy to Restoration* (Salt Lake City: Deseret Book, 1960), 227–28.
3. Alexander of Hales, quoted in Mosheim, *Ecclesiastical History*, 3:4.
4. Barker, *Apostasy*, 729.
5. Ibid.
6. Schaff, *A History of the Christian Church*, vol. 7, 241, quoted in Barker, *Apostasy*, 729; emphasis added.
7. Ibid., 756.
8. Ibid., 757–58.
9. Vicki Jo Anderson, *The Other Eminent Men of Wilford Woodruff* (Cottonwood, AZ: Zichron Historical Research Institute, 1994), 381–82.
10. Through a modern prophet and president of The Church of Jesus Christ of Latter-day Saints, Wilford Woodruff, it was revealed that John Wesley, as well as a number of other prominent men and women of earlier times, was taught and had accepted the pure gospel of Jesus Christ while dwelling in the spirit world. Although it is not specifically taught as official Church doctrine, I share a personal opinion and belief with many other LDS members that Wesley continues to use his highly virtuous character and many God-given talents in preaching the pure gospel of Jesus Christ in the spirit world even today. This is likely true of many of the other early Reformers as well.
11. Anderson, *The Other Eminent Men of Wilford Woodruff*, 387.
12. Bruce R. McConkie, *Mormon Doctrine*, 2nd ed. (Salt Lake City: Bookcraft, 1966), 338.
13. Bible Dictionary, "grace," 697.
14. Hyrum L. Andrus, *God, Man and the Universe*, 206, quoted in Robert L. Millet, *By Grace Are We Saved* (Salt Lake City: Bookcraft, 1989), 40.

Conclusion

As people study the original, pure teachings of Christ as found within The Church of Jesus Christ of Latter-day Saints, they discover that God is a much, much different Being from the one commonly portrayed in the modern Christian world. They learn that God does not physically torture infants, children, and adults by forever burning their flesh with fire. He does not eternally condemn a man or woman for not accepting a gospel they never even knew existed. He does not randomly bestow His grace and the blessings of salvation upon one person, while purposely and unfairly withholding these same blessings from another. He does not force a man or woman to either heaven or hell. If these and so many other unreasonable teachings of modern Christianity were actually true, who would even want to live in the presence of such a cruel, unjust, and merciless Being?

What a blessing it is to understand the true, loving nature of God. As we study the teachings of the restored church and gospel of Jesus Christ, we will find our questions about God and His divine plan of salvation finally answered in ways that actually make sense.

Many people are quite shocked when they learn of the tremendous differences between the teachings of ancient, original Christianity and the teachings of modern Christianity. Perhaps you have been more than a little surprised yourself.

For the sake of brevity, only eleven simple examples have been cited here, but these are not isolated cases. Actually, dozens more examples of a similar nature might have easily been cited, each one clearly illustrating the total loss or extreme perversion of original Christian doctrines and practices that took place during medieval times and continue to occur in modern times.

As each of us seeks the blessings of salvation, we must ever be mindful that the pathway leading to God's presence is not built upon a foundation of human speculations and superstitions, man-made doctrines, and half-Christian, half-pagan rituals and philosophies. Rather, this path is built upon a foundation of pure and undefiled truth. In speaking of this true path, the Savior declared, "For wide is the gate, and broad is the way, that leadeth to destruction, and *many* there be which go in thereat: Because strait is the gate, and narrow is the way, which leadeth unto life, and *few* there be that find it" (Matthew 7:13–14; italics added).

Unfortunately, the reason that so few will ever find and enter the true gate leading to eternal life in God's presence is not because it is impossible to discover or does not exist. It is simply because there are few individuals who are humbly, prayerfully, and actively searching for it! Sadly, most people will not be interested in Christ's message; many will be offended by it; some will spread lies and actively fight against it. The great challenge to each of us, of course, is to be among the relatively few of whom the Savior spoke, who have sufficiently prepared their hearts and minds to recognize this perfect, true gospel for what it really is—and then to actively make it the center of their lives.

THE TRUTH IS RESTORED

Although the Savior's teachings were greatly corrupted during the Middle and Dark Ages, I hope you clearly understand that because of Heavenly Father's love for you, He has made certain that you, and all of His other children, will be given the opportunity to hear His true gospel message. The opportunity for an individual to hear this true message may come in this life, or it may come in the next life during one's stay in the spirit world. But no matter when it may come, rest assured it *will* come.

We are so blessed in our day to have Christ's pure gospel available to us. Unlike so many others, we don't have to wait until the next life to receive it! However, with this blessing comes a great responsibility. The Lord has indicated that those living on earth who have received sufficient opportunity to clearly understand and accept His true gospel, but who reject it or who do not faithfully live it, will not be given a second chance to qualify for eternal life while in the spirit world. Why not? Because living one's life forever in the Father's presence is reserved for only His most valiant children, not for those who are unbelieving, half-committed or lukewarm, or who would purposely procrastinate the day of their repentance. Thus, how very critical it is that each of us embrace and faithfully live this true gospel while on earth if given the chance to do so.

Of course, those who reject or who do not faithfully live Christ's true gospel while here on earth can still qualify for a lesser degree of glory in the next life. But remember that eternity is a very long time. Would anyone really want to live forever in a state of happiness that is comparable to the glory and brightness of the moon when, with a little more effort, they could qualify to live eternally in a state of happiness comparable to the glory and brightness of the sun? Or, as another way of illustrating this difference, figuratively speaking, would you like to receive four thousand dollars or would you rather receive eighty million dollars as an eternal inheritance from your Father? Is it worth the effort to qualify for a life in your Heavenly Father's actual presence? Without a doubt!

Now, it is my witness to you, dear reader, that the Lord's true gospel exists today within the church that the Savior Himself reestablished upon the earth, within The Church of Jesus Christ of Latter-day Saints. In describing this restored church and gospel of Jesus Christ, a modern-day apostle wrote,

> This newly organized Church is the same in every essential particular as the Church of the Lamb has been in all ages when it has been found among men. It conforms, for instance, to the New Testament pattern of the Lord's Church. In it is found the same authority, the same organization, the same ordinances, the same teachings and doctrines that were found in the primitive Church. And the same gifts of the Spirit—revelations, visions, miracles, healings, the ministering of angels, tongues, and a host of others—as were poured out upon the ancient saints are again showered in equal measure upon the modern saints, the members of the Lord's own Church and Kingdom.[1]

The pure and undefiled church and gospel of Jesus Christ is available to you and to me, and indeed to any and to all who will humbly and sincerely seek it.

My Testimony to You

Now, may the Lord bless you, dear friend, in your search for pure and undefiled truth. May I leave you with my humble and most sincere testimony that I do know, even as I know that I live, that God lives and loves us so very much. I know that our Heavenly Father did not place you and me upon the earth without a divine plan in mind for us. I also know that a clear understanding of that plan, major portions of which were corrupted and lost during the Middle and Dark Ages, has been restored to earth.

I further testify to you, dear reader, that God loves His children who are alive upon the earth today just as much as He has loved His children in ages past. He has not forgotten us. It is my most sincere belief and solemn witness to you that He has lifted the clouds of confusion, which have engulfed the world for so many centuries, by once again calling and revealing His pure gospel to a latter-day prophet—the Prophet Joseph Smith.

Having been a student of the life and teachings of the Prophet Joseph Smith for many, many years, I can declare without any reservation whatsoever that I do know that he was indeed a true prophet of God. Unlike the teachings of any other church or individual, I have found his teachings to be in complete harmony with the teachings of Christ as taught in the days of the ancient apostles. Unlike so many of the teachings of modern Christendom, Joseph's teachings are actually reasonable and make sense. In his teachings there are no unbaptized babies who burn and are forever physically tortured in hellfire; no random bestowal of saving grace upon a fortunate few based upon nothing more than some divine whim or sheer luck; no lukewarm and half-committed individuals that dwell in our Father's presence; and certainly there is no belief in a Christ who prays for hours and even for days at a time to Himself and then finally decides to answers His own prayers. Nor are there any other teachings or doctrines that can be traced directly back to pagan rituals, man-made inventions, and ancient Greek philosophies in what he taught. Why not? Because he received his teachings directly from the source of all truth, even from God Himself.

Even greater than the intellectual conviction I have received from the study of this prophet's teachings is the deep spiritual conviction I have received from the witness of the Spirit. For I have spent much time on my knees in humble prayer before God, seeking to know of a certainty if what I have learned is true. In all sincerity and solemnity, I wish you to know that I have received a witness deep in my heart and mind, born of the Holy Ghost, that Joseph Smith was indeed a true prophet and that what he taught is of God. I bear witness to you that if you will follow this same process of carefully studying and then sincerely praying to God to know if these things are true, God will manifest the truth of it to you through the power of the Holy Ghost.

Perhaps you are wondering how the Holy Ghost can let a person know of the truth of something they have been taught. We have an example in the New Testament of how two of Jesus' disciples knew that what He was teaching them was true. After walking and talking with these two men and then having shared supper with them, the Savior left. Now alone together, the scriptural account of the conversation of these men records, "And they said one to another, Did not our heart burn within us, while he [Christ] talked with us by the way, and while he opened to us the scriptures?" (Luke 24:32).

Although a witness of the Spirit to one's heart and mind is extremely difficult to explain in words, these particular disciples experienced it as a burning sensation in their heart. Some describe it as a tingly sensation they feel traveling through their mind and body—somewhat like having the shivers except without feeling cold. For others it often manifests itself as a feeling of profound peace or joy that totally envelops their mind and heart. As you humbly, sincerely, and fervently pray to God to know the truth, be conscious of such feelings from the Spirit. They are provided by God to testify to your heart and mind that what you have been taught is true.

As we come to the end of our time together, dear friend, perhaps you can now understand why our young LDS missionaries are not only willing, but eager, to give two years of their lives in service to the Lord. For they have a message sent directly from God to give to all other humble seekers of truth. Indeed, it is by far the greatest and most important message existing anywhere upon the face of the earth.

As you prayerfully read the Book of Mormon, you will come to know for a certainty that Jesus is indeed the Christ, that Joseph Smith was truly a prophet of God, and that Christ's true church and gospel really do exist once again upon the earth today. As you attend church and gain a testimony of its truth, I promise you will learn all that you must do to return to the presence of your loving Heavenly Father.

Now, dear friend, may you prove to be among those relatively few special souls of whom the Savior spoke, who are sincerely seeking Him and His pure gospel. May you be among those few valiant souls who are actively seeking that third heaven that the apostle Paul saw. May you find the truth and happiness you seek, and may the Lord bless you in all of your righteous endeavors. This is my most humble prayer, in the name of our beloved Lord and Savior, Jesus the Christ. Amen.

NOTES

1. McConkie, *Mormon Doctrine*, 137.

About the Author

Gregory R. Wille was born and raised in Chicago, Illinois. Growing up, he played Little League baseball and high school basketball, and earned his Eagle Scout award. As a young man he served a full-time LDS mission to Australia and afterward graduated from BYU with a degree in accounting. He met his eternal companion, Shelley, in a BYU ward, and they were married in the Salt Lake Temple. They are the parents of two daughters and four sons and are currently grandparents to seven very active little grandchildren. Their six children have served missions to England, Norway, Ukraine, France, Australia, and Mexico.

Brother Wille has worked for a CPA firm, a large international oil company, and several other smaller firms, as an accountant, administrative coordinator, and chief financial officer. He has also served in many teaching and leadership positions in the Church. Next to his love for God and the Savior, his greatest joy comes in knowing that families are forever.